Hook-up Chronicles

Volume 1

Hook-up Chronicles

by Chelsea Goldstein

© 2009 by ChelseaMedia

© 2009 by ChelseaMedia

All rights reserved, except as permitted under the U.S. Copyright Act of 1976. No part of this publication may be reproduced, distributed, or transmitted in any form or by any means, or stored in a database or retrieval system, without the prior written permission of the publisher.

ChelseaMedia
P.O. Box 30068
Kansas City, MO 64112

www.chelseagoldstein.com

Author's note: The events described in these stories are real, although the names and other identifying characteristics have been changed to protect the innocent and guilty alike.

ISBN: 1-4392-4883-4

Library of Congress Control Number: 2009906865

Printed in The United States of America

ACKNOWLEDGEMENT

To the Women who have trusted me with their secrets, and are willing to share to their most personal expeiences with the world.

INTRODUCTION

To say that American women are liberated is an insult. We were never enslaved. Neither were our mothers, for that matter. While we may only be a few generations from the male dominated American society in the history books, today's modern American women have never experienced a world in which they were not free to pursue their own happiness. That said, we were never taught exactly how to do that.

It is one thing to be free under the law, it's quite another to be free in mind. To really be empowered to pursue happiness requires the pursuer to be free to choose any path that might lead her there. Taboo, social more and peer pressure can be powerful limiting factors that work invisibly to prevent people from finding real happiness.

For generations, American women have been told, both explicitly and implicitly, that sexual pleasure was the man's path to happiness and unsuitable for modern women. A woman who enjoyed sex and pursued it for enjoyment's sake was labeled a slut, a whore or worse. Women were told to seek sexual ecstasy only within the framework of a loving marriage, while men were free to seek it out where ever they could find it.

Those days are ending. The stories in this volume are testament to that fact. In the pages that follow, you will hear first hand the tales of women-possibly just like you-who have overcome the stereotypes and risked their reputations in the pursuit of passion, excitement, and entertainment.

In preparing this material for publishing, I learned that women today are empowered to fulfill their own sexual fantasies, to go beyond the daydream and throw themselves into sexual exploration. In story after story, the strong voices of women everywhere cried out in defiance of the invisible bonds that held them back, in unbridled joy as they rushed headlong into new erotic worlds and, finally, in ecstasy as they earned the reward for living life fully.

These stories will change how you look at the women around you,and how you feel about yourself. As yu imagine these adventures, pehaps you will recount your own, or vow to have an adventure of your own!

Sincerely,

Chelsea Goldstein
www.chelseagoldstein.com

Hook-up Chronicles

Volume 1

Vixen

by Jessica S. – Livingston, NJ, age 27

A couple of years ago, an "anonymous" vixen dressed up as a sexy cab driver for a Halloween party. After hours of dancing with her girlfriends, she found a very attractive caveman and hit it off instantly.

This girl was feeling particularly naughty and decided to go home with him but not with out her overnight bag. She made him drive from the party to the friend's house to get the bag, then drop her friend off across town at another mans house, and finally back to his house. By that time, the two had made out at every stoplight along the way and the passion was mounting.

It was like a scene out of a movie, each piece of clothing including her driving gloves and checkered thigh highs torn from her body and strewn from the foyer, up the stairs, through the hallway and into the bed room, where the two gave into pure animal lust.

Morning comes: "Where the hell am I?" she wonders peering through crusty fake eyelashes at the unfamiliar bedroom. The smell of stale booze hangs in the air and she thinks, "Get me out of here". Frantically collecting each item along the path from the bedroom to the foot of the stairs, she stuffs them into her overnight bag, and puts on her pajamas, which incidentally were never worn.

Friend answers phone and agrees to pick her up. She feels a combination of feelings regret for giving into desire so shamelessly the night before, but also triumph for being comfortable with her sexuality it was entirely liberating. Unfortunately, she forgot to pack a change of shoes, and was forced to go to breakfast with her friend in stilettos and pajamas not the least bit embarrassing.

A few months later, the vixen finds herself flying to Florida for another opportunity to dress up as Gasparilla. One of her friends is on the same flight. The two couldn't sit next to each other, but rather, one in front of the other. She looks up other options one seat is open in the emergency exit row 13E. Hmmmm... Switch and have more leg room or stay and be able to converse with friend? She decides to leave things alone.

She and her friend go to the airport, looking forward to trip ahead. As the pair board the plane, she surveys the passengers, hoping to be seated next to an attractive male. Then she meets eyes with Caveman, sitting in 13D. "Thank God I did not switch seats," she thinks to herself as she makes her way back to 18E. His gaze burns into her as she walks by, smiling to herself. He didn't look half as good in a suit as he did as a caveman.

She passes a note to her friend behind her to let her in on the laugh, she can't help but wonder what would have happened if she HAD switched seats. Would she have been the newest member of the mile high club? Or would it have been the most painful plane ride of her life? She shook her head, laughed, and began to imagine all of the mischief she would get into upon her arrival in Florida.

The List

by Nicole W. – Ottawa, IL, age 27

Anyways, I am a born again Christian, so none of this stuff counts anymore. However here are my slutty moments. In list form.

1. I had a crush on two of my social studies teachers and was crushed when I found out one of them got married.

2. I was secretly pleased when I found out Chipper Jones cheated on his wife because I thought, "Chipper cheats on his wife, now I actually have a shot with this guy."

3. I lost my virginity to a guy I met on the internet.

4. I went to third base with another guy I met off the internet.

5. I've read Craigslist and know what m4w means.

6. Slutty by proxy: I was in the same room while my friend got knocked up with another man's baby while she was married.

7. That same night I jumped on a trampoline in my Eskimo costume. You could see my underwear.

Yes, I was wearing them. I'm not easy you know.

8. And then went to third base with a guy dressed up as a killer farmer for Halloween.

9. I have given a guy at a club my real number.

10. I stayed at a club after my friends had left.

11. I was at a club when they turned the lights on.

12. I spooned an atheist.

13. Slutty by proxy: Two of my high school friends have venereal diseases. I don't really talk to them anymore though.

14. I threw up and cried at a friend's house. That same night our manorexic friend started crying too and told everyone he didn't eat.

15. I made out with a married guy

16. Who was black.

17. Okay, I had sex with him too.

18. I used to wear low cut dresses to church.

19. I assumed this guy liked me even though he was dating someone so I made out with him just to make sure that my assumptions were correct.

20. I made out with a high school kid when I was 26 years old.

21. I touched my first penis in a dog house. The penis belonged to my babysitter's son. We were the same age. Don't judge: no laws were broken.

22. I took a picture of my friend while she was using the bathroom.

23. I spent the night at some dude's house I had never met. Not only was I slutty that night, I guess I

was feeling rapey too.

24. I think Bob Saget from Full House is sexy and I might make out with him.

25. I have always wanted to have sex while wearing a miniskirt with ruffles on it.

26. If you are a man in an authoritative position, I have wanted you.

27. I want a man to slap me. Just one time though, nothing Montel Williams crazy.

28. I wear tampons.

Vicodin

by Rebecca R. – California, PA, age 21

After the show my friends and I went bar hopping. Well somewhere in between a few Vicodin and God knows how many drinks I made out with more then seven different men. According to my friends after watching me act like a slut with a few they started taking pictures because I do not even believe half the shit I do. So low and behold the next day they showed me locking lips and getting dry humped by seven different guys. Good times

Chelsea Goldstein – www.chelseagoldstein.com

In the Snow

by Catherine T. – Champaign, IL, age 20

I was drunk at a party. It was pretty crowded inside so I went on the front porch. I started talking to this guy that I didn't know who I could barely see because it was so dark and within 10 seconds we were making out. He took my hand and dragged me behind the house. It was completely dark out and the ground was covered with snow.

I took off my jacket. Then we went to two houses over behind a shed, we did not know the people who owned this shed. I took off my pants and boots and climbed on top of him and we started having sex behind a stranger's house, with my bare feet in the freezing snow.

After a while, my feet were frozen and I started getting tired, he had whiskey dick so it didn't look like he was finishing anytime soon. So I got off him and gave him a bj, trying to make him cum but it was taking forever. So then I was like fuck it I got go and left him in the snow with his boner, he was pissed. That was the night I lost my virginity.

Flatulence

by Tiffany A. – Norman, OK, age 34

Back in my freak days I am retired freak now that I'm in a relationship I went to a local Norman bar we will call the nugget. That is seriously the name after 100 shots of patron I was feeling a little randy, so I start peeping out dudes. My eyes become fixated on the DJ, DJ Ice if you want to know his name.

So we talk and I guess he figured out I was willing to give him some, because he invited me back to his place when his gig was through. We get to his place and proceed with the foreplay, when he notices that I had started my period. You know how you think your done, but your not well it didn't seem to bother him and after 200 shots of Patron and some Vicodin I didn't care either.

So we proceed with the deed and 1 minute into he farts the loudest fart you ever heard, well needless to say I can not deal and from that moment on DJ Ice became DJ flatulence, and I made sure everyone in the club scene in Norman knew it.

Chocolate

by Erika B. – Philadelphia, PA, age 19

This story involved me and a group of my close friends at college in Philadelphia. It was last year and my friends and I decided to go to a "red light party." Most of us had never heard of this kind of party, but our black friends said it was big around here. It's basically just a party at a house and there is a red light on the front porch to show you where the party is at kind of dumb, I know.

So anyway we all decided to go and we arrived at this party like 11ish. We open the door and there are about 6 people there. Me and my friend's Crystal and Courtney were the only white people in the house. I immediately went to get alcohol because if this party stayed the way it was, someone would have to get drunk and make a fool of them self to lighten up the mood. I walk up to the bar in the kitchen and 10 minutes later I had downed 26 Jello Shots, 2 regular shots of Jack Daniels and 3 hits of weed from a man who walked out of the bathroom.

I walked back out to the party and it was PACKED with me Crystal and Courtney still being the only white people there. I immediately started doing the drunken white girl dance, waving my arms over my head and bopping along not on beat with the music. Apparently this is attractive to black men because in a matter of seconds I was smashed against a wall with a beautiful chocolate boy literally on top of me dancing. I was pretty much passing out on him so he propped me against a wall for support.

Somehow during the course of the night I lost my top and found it on top of a fridge, which then tempted me to have more Jello shots. Multiple times I wound up upstairs in a bedroom with the chocolate boy, but each time my loving friends were kind enough to barge in with some nice words such as "Erika, come back downstairs", "don't have sex", and "where's your wallet, we need money to buy hot dogs at 7-Eleven".

As the night came to an end, we exchanged numbers and I went back downstairs to find my fellow people. Crystal had hooked up with a 26-year old ex coke dealer who just got out of jail 5 days ago. As we were walking out I spotted a black friend of mine and proceeded to ask her if I could use her cover-up, to which she replied "youze iz madd drunk foo."

This may not have been the juiciest story but it's definitely one me and my friends will remember... sort of.

Elevator

by Katherine L. – Hartford, CT, age 18

I was on vacation in the Bahamas with some friends. My current boyfriend, Zach, was dating my good friend, who was also on the trip. Before me and Zach started going out, it was obvious that we were both into each other, but neither one of us ever dared to say anything because he was going out with my friend, and they say friends' boyfriends are off limits.

So for a year, I guess we tried to ignore this mutual attraction. One night, our whole group of friends went out to a club. We had a really great time of what I can remember, but I had a little too much to drink so I said I needed to go back to the hotel. Zach offered to go with me, admitting that he also may have had a bit too much to drink. His girlfriend did not mind him going with me because she never suspected that we would be even remotely attracted to each other.

After we stumbled into the lobby of the hotel together, we walked into the elevator. It was just Zach and I in the elevator. Well, as destiny would have it, the elevator broke down. We got on the emergency phone and were surprised to hear from the maintenance repairman that it would take about an hour and a half to fix. Well that was the end to our "silent" attraction.

We started talking about how we had always liked each other and that his interest in his girl-friend had faded a while back. We started making out for about ten minutes. Then we decided to take advantage of the hour plus that we still had alone in the elevator, so we started having sex. The sex was great and we were both very into it. Zach and I were still naked on the elevator floor having sex when the elevator door opened.

We were so surprised because it had been fixed in 30 minutes, not the 90 minutes the maintenance guy had estimated. Looking in at us were about 15 people waiting to get in the elevator. You don't think it could get any worse? Among those 15 people were a few of our friends, including Zach's girlfriend. So basically that was the end of our friendship, but only the beginning of me and Zach's relationship. We have been dating for a while now and we are very happy. Thankfully, his ex never shared that story with the public because what I did was so unlike me. But I am happy it happened!

Blue Balls

by Kathryn E. – Los Angeles, CA, age 23

My roommate and I went over to her boyfriend's house to hang out, drink, and have a good time. We planned on it being nice and relaxed, but when we showed up I realized that her boyfriend had also invited a friend, Justin, and he was just my type. My roommate is the most innocent girl you will ever meet. She is 22, a virgin, and has posters up in her room of "Harry Potter" and "High School Musical". Her and her boyfriend have been going out for a year and he is constantly crying to me about his blue balls, sexual frustrations with the fact that my roommate won't put out, and his secret desire for anal sex.

Anyway, we drank the night away playing a crazy game of Kings and I ended up having a grand ole time making out with not only Justin, but my roommate too. At this point her boyfriend begged her to sneak away to make out with him which is all they ever do and left me and Justin alone to get to know each other. Well, we ended up sneaking into my room-

Hook-up Chronicles   Vol. 1

mate's boyfriend's room and ravaging each other. He flipped me over the side of the bed and had me in all these crazy positions I had never even been in before. He was trying to talk dirty, and in order to keep myself from laughing I just moaned really loudly. He was telling me things like, "I love rubbing your soft pillows" and "You make me hard as a rocket" and other equally lame things like that. It was crazy and intense, but I was trying to hurry before they caught us because the lock didn't work on the door.

The second I orgasmed my roommate banged on the door and told me to hurry up. I apologized to Justin for the blue balls, threw on my clothes, and ran out of the house with my roommate in tow. I told her nothing happened and drove us home. Poor Justin was left in the bed, naked, and unable to explain himself to his confused and horrified friend.

Prison Tat

by Allison C. – Boston, MA, age 42

I am thirty something at a gay bar hosting a Sandra Bernhardt after party in Boston. I am offered coke in the bathroom by a big boned Barbie tranny. Then some Babson girls chop up some Ritalin. Why not? During all this, I lost my friend Joe. Or Joe lost me to make out in a photo booth.

It is the end of the night. Things close at 2 am in Boston, and they kick you out before that. I am standing on the stage, scouting the place for Joe. "You are very pretty," a very young guy says to me. "Oh you mean for a woman?" "I like women!" "How nice for your mother..." "No--I mean, I am bisexual." "How nice for everyone." And so it went for awhile.

We walked out together Joe is long gone and sat on the edge of the Fence during the day, a popular jogging and basketball area by night, a whole different kind of exercise yard. I made him show me his id because he was so young looking he had been trying to grow a mustache, but it was like a dusting of

Downey fuzz. Not hot in the least. He was 19. I told him I was a lot older than him not being presumptuous since he'd already told me he wanted to go home with me. He said, "I like older women. My first time was with an older woman. I was 13 and she was 18." I already knew from his id that he was from Florida, so I had to ask. "Did you grow up in a trailer park or something?" He looked truly hurt. "Yes."

It was getting later, and I decided it would be easier to let him come home with me I lived 6 blocks away than to try to get rid of him. I am a giver. I did tell him that if he came home with me, he had to shave his mustache off. We get into the shower and swear to God, the kid has a tattoo on his back, home made no less, and he got it, you guessed it in prison! That reads:

W
SEX
T

Baseball

by Maria E. – Miami, FL, age 21

This guy and I had a extremely flirtatious relationship all throughout high school but we never officially dated or fooled around. He was an all star baseball player about to go away to college on scholarship. It was right before graduation and everyone in our class decided to camp and party on school grounds as the senior prank.

I currently had a boyfriend who was older and was not invited to shit shindig. My current boyfriend showed up and I hangout in his car for awhile and made out. But I knew I could not leave with him because there was serious heat between me and the baseball man. I knew something was going to go down. So I stayed. About two hours and 8 beers later, me and baseball man were sitting together making out in front of everyone.

For more privacy we started walking out toward the baseball field and made our way to the dugout. After messing around there for a while we decided to head right to the middle of the baseball field. As you could probably predict, he scored a home run. Right on 3rd base!

Country Clubbing

by Vanessa P. – Lexington-Fayette, KY, age 22

One night several years ago my friend and I decide it sounds like a good idea to meet up with two guys we know at our towns Country Club. The Country Club is closed and it is about 1 A.M., but since the people in our town are too trusting of others and also moronic, the building where the golf carts are stored is left open at all times.

Because we know we have two hotties waiting on us near the pool area at the Club, we decide its a good idea to slut it up a little bit and we wear the shortest cotton skirts we own along with halter tops so skimpy that there really is not a need to wear strapless bras but we did, however. To this day I'm not sure why in the hell we thought we would look cute in those outfits, but they seem to have done the trick.

I say this because when we got there the guys were leaning against Josh's (Guy 1, my chosen hookup for the night) champagne colored Infiniti, both trying to look as sly as one can look in a Titlist visor and golf shoes. Why we did not realize these guys probably did not swing our way off the course at the time still baffles me.

My friend had barely spoken the word hello when Stephen (Guy 2, her chosen hookup) whisked her away to the pool area, leaving me standing in the parking lot looking like a prostitute as I thought of something witty to say to Josh. But before I could come up with anything, he asked me about my day at work.

I was working at his parent's jewelry store that year before I left to go to college, so this topic seemed safe for us. His mom was a regular Stepford wife, only worse since we were in the heart of Kentucky and every Stepford wife there behaved as if it were still 1958 and the mile high hair tease was a glorious new development.

I was sure that if she could see me now, standing in the parking lot of the local Country Club and whoring it out in front of her oldest son, shed be unpleasantly surprised to say the least.

To break the ice, Josh asked me if I wanted to go sit with him in a golf cart. Hoping this was his code line for sex, I happily followed, stilettos clacking on the pavement. Once we got in the garage, he grabbed my breasts quickly and sloppily began to kiss me up and down my neck. Josh was a hot guy, so his lack of skill in the bedroom arena surprised me. Eventually, he unzipped his khaki shorts and I decided that if I went down under he be likely to at least return the favor for the rest of the night.

When I got into the game area, I learned a lot about Josh in a short amount of time. For one, he was not very well endowed. Secondly, he was one of those aggressive types who like to have his hand on your head and perform the back and forth motions for you, which annoyed the hell out of me and also made me choke.

Hold up, I said, you got to stop doing that shit or I'm going to stop the performance here, I warned him. But as I continued, his hand did not stop pushing against my head. I had had a little too much to drink that night already, so once I started gagging, it did not take long for the Zimas to come right back up and onto his package. Luckily, he was drunk too and thought he had finished at the exact moment. I am pretty sure he figured out what had really happened later on in his life, but at the time I did not care. He needed to learn it was not okay to push when a girl was doing you one big favor or small favor, in his case.

About two months later I was in the back of the jewelry store and had just returned back to work from a hiatus after having my wisdom teeth removed, resulting in dry sockets in all four holes. To my horror, Josh's mom walked in, followed by Josh himself. Josh's about to have his wisdom teeth taken out. I told him that you had the scoop on it since you just had yours removed, she smiled grandly, looking from her son to me. My face turned bright red and Josh hesitantly stared at the floor. I had four dry sockets, Josh, His mother announced, eyebrows raised at him in warning, they say not to suck on straws or anything in the week that follows the surgery, but she did not listen. I quickly turned and exited for the bathroom around that time, and by the time I came back, he was gone.

Last week I saw on Facebook where Josh was engaged to a girl who looks exactly like his mother and I could not help but wonder if he pushes her head also during oral sex, and if he does what she does as payback.

Drill Sergeant

by Shannon N. – APO, AE, age 21

So I am in the Army and I think after going through Boot camp it is every female soldiers dream to hookup with one of her Drill Sergeants. They are scary mean guys you always see screaming in someone's face in Army movies. I got sent to Germany on an assignment and end up getting in touch with one of my Drill Sergeants through email.

Long story short, I bought a plane ticket to stay in North Carolina for one day to hook up with this guy. Great sex, but worth $1000? Probably not. Plane ticket to North Carolina $800, Hotel for one night $100, Being able to say I fucked a Drill Sergeant, Honest to God Priceless!

Magnum

by Andrea H. – Fairfield, CT, age 23

I went to Vegas in June with my three girlfriends and when we arrived we headed straight to for the liquor store. Also we stopped and ate some Sonic too. On the way to our booze, I had said I want some hotties. I brought condoms, to which my friends replied, "Andrea, you seriously brought condoms?" "Ummm HELL YEA I did - Magnums, bitches!" They started dying of laughter and said they admired me for it, but why Magnums, what if they don not fit? To which I stated, "If they do not fit, keep it moving, because you are not going to do anything for me anyway." I was told, "This is why you are my best friend" by my girlfriend Lisa.

We stayed three nights and four days and no such booty luck and I was pissed. Finally, on the last night, we stayed in the hotel the Palms and went to Rain. That blew, so we went to Ghost Bar and me and my girlfriend Jen and Jamie managed to talk to a very nice group of guys that said, "Hey we have a suite upstairs because my boy had his bachelor party, want to come up?" I obviously had no problem saying yea, so I took this guy's number down and proceeded to down my Goose and Cranberry. You got to watch out for those UTI's, you know.

I called the dudes and he gave us the room number. Now the room number sounded familiar and I was confused. Was I that fucked up that I had already been here? No, it was the Real World suite.

So my girlfriend and I decided to go in. About 15 to 20 people might have been in there playing pool, getting naked and going in the hot tub, drinking, and etc. I found the bar, then a sexy man and decided to straddle him and make out with him. I wish I caught his name though. Got up and saw this cute little nugget of a man. He mentions something risqué to me, and me being my horny self that had been trying to get laid all weekend, responded with, "do not tempt me cause I will take you away and bang you right now." That is when he took my hand, I looked back at my friend and she was laughing on the lap of this sexy cop. That was actually the cousin of my little man. We ended up in the confessional on the floor. I looked at him and said, "I only have magnums", and he said, "Oh that's quite alright." YES, thank God. I proceeded to rock his world until I heard Jamie calling my name. FUCK! FUCK! NO! I couldn't let her walk back to her room all alone all the way in the new Palms Place tower. So after hearing my name and knowing they were looking for us we had to stop. He said, you better be coming back, and I responded I will. He told me I was really good and I said oh I know thanks. He then proceeded to tell me he had a fiancée. I slapped his face and walked out. So I dropped Jamie off at the room, and came back.

HE WAS GONE! Mother fucker! There now were not really any people in the suite. I looked in one of the bedrooms and found my girl Jen on top of this dude making out with him. The loser never even had sex with him, and man was he fine. But there was a bed next to theirs with a boy in it. I hadn't seen him earlier but I said hi! He had no problem saying hi back and saying, "You can come in here and lay I won't touch you." I laughed at him and climbed in. We actually laid there for an hour laughing hysterically at random things and our friends hooking up next to us, and not having sex very lame.

I even got his name, Chris. Obviously we ended up making out and getting naked and I was poking around his penis. Which unfortunately was not as big as the random man's before. But whatever, I said I can't do this next to my friend. Even though at this time now they were sleeping.

We heard people still out there partying, but I snuck out wrapped up in a blanket with my new guy. We went to the confessional room. There was a condom on the bathroom counter so he grabbed it and ducked back in the confessional room.

There I was on the floor again. I did not think the magnum would fit, and my plan of shooting a man down was gone at this point, because I wanted to finish what I started. Went thru that whole magnum ordeal, it basically fit, it was not baggy so here we go. We had sex for a while. He actually liked my love locket and spent plenty of time down there. Dumb ass, I just banged your friend, and you do not know. The condom dried up, damn latex, so I was like fuck! He pulled out, went down on me some more, and then we realized that the condom was gone! WTF Where is it. We figured that it just fell off when he pulled out and was going down on me.

We looked around the floor of the confessional room, but gave up. He opened the door to look, and OBVIOUSLY there was one on the bathroom counter so he grabbed it and ducked back in the confessional room. I had wished I known the condom on the counter had existed before I attempted the magnum condom.

We continued to have sex and it pretty good for my drunken ass. I preferred it from behind considering he wasn't that big, that felt the best. But then we heard a dude outside snorting everywhere. Like hawking up loogies and blowing his nose. We looked at each other and laughed and finally gave up because the mood was gone. I was whatever cause he went down on me, bitch. We were both SO fucked up we just got up. He never got off, nor do I care. I woke up Jen up, we left.

It was 9:30 a.m., we looked like dirty whores traipsing around the Palms in our clothes and make up and stilettos from the night before. We obviously got some McDonald's and eat it in our bathroom in our room, as not to wake the other two girls. We took a 2 hour nap, packed and checked out, went to the pool, laid there and got a bucket o' beers and a tall goose and OJ and Cranberry. We had a red eye, so we had all day to fart around. We had dinner reservations and N9NE Steakhouse at 6 p.m.

We went back to the lobby of our hotel, had the bell boy get our bags, grabbed some presentable clothes, and went to the lobby bathroom to change into them for dinner. OH GOD. I am in the bathroom stall. I go pee and I push a little. I am like WTF? I don't have a tampon in? All of a sudden it hits me. OH GOD OH GOD OH GOD NO. I cringed and closed my eyes and stuck my hand down and pulled out A FUCKING MAGNUM CONDOM OUT OF MY PRECIOUS LITTLE LOVE LOCKET. I started to gag and dry heave a little. My body had chills all over it, and does not as I'm recapping this. I flushed it down the toilet. Swung open the bathroom door grabbed and shitload of paper towels with soap and water and ran back in there and sat, basically twisting the paper towel in my damn birthing canal.

I was so grossed out. I could not tell my girlfriends, so I did not. I did however call my best friend at home and let her proceed to laugh. My only savior was that the poor guy never came. Thank God. But I had just a condom in my vagina for almost 12 hours!! Just sitting there, chilling, oh God ewwwwwwwwww. I knew the magnum did not fit but it did not seem huge on it, I guess the vigorous thrusting pulled it off, ughhhhhhh!

I got laid in Vegas twice in one night in the same room with two different men amazingly awesome. I also had a condom lost in my vagina for 12 hours. I got tested. I am fine, just very traumatized.

His Wife

by Lauren M. – Ann Arbor, MI, age 34

Two girlfriends and I had a pretty major girl's night out and went to a dance club. We danced and drank the night away. Guys were buying us drinks left and right, it was awesome! My ex boyfriend showed up whom to this day I have a strong attraction to and we ended up having a good time dancing with him. He fed us even more drinks. It got pretty sexual out on the dance floor with all of us. I could feel his hard on every time we danced.

He is known as "the Trunk" by all of my friends from when we were dating. By this time, we were all completely shit faced. We left the club at closing time and I invited everyone back to my mom's with us as I had an apartment in her basement what a loser.

I had no idea what was about to happen but I was wasted and did not want the party to end there. We drove back all shitty wasted. I have no idea how we even made it back. After some talking and laughing trying our best to be quiet so my mom would not hear us, the girls and I ended up play fighting. It was sort of like a silly girl "Wrestle Mania" that got started. This led to the ex boyfriend telling us to kiss which we did. It was all happening so fast I hardly had time to even think. It is not like my head was clear anyway. I thought "fuck it" lets go this. He got all excited and somehow got involved in it which I was happy about because I was a little awkward as it was my first time kissing a girl.

We were all making out in the living room and getting really frisky so I decided it would be a good idea to take it to the bedroom. I did not get any arguments. We all stripped down naked and got hot and heavy in my bed. Eventually it turned into my two friends having sex and the ex and I having sex. After I got bored with him, I started making out with the girls again. One of them who I did not know as well as the other one took me out of the bedroom and back into the living room where she proceeded to do things to my Pikachu that to this day I have never had done before.

My other friend ended up screwing the ex but I did not care, I could not even see straight. This chick had major talent which probably came from the fact that she was a lesbian I later found out. The ex proceeded to bang my friend silly while I let this chick have her way with me. I did nothing but enjoy myself and forget about whatever else was going on. When she was done, we went back into the bedroom and everyone was pretty happy and tired too so I kicked their asses out. I got mine and I was ready for some sleep.

That is and probably always will be the sluttish thing I've ever done. I ran into the ex with his wife a few months ago this summer. It was really quite awkward but it is the first thing I thought of when I saw him. I wondered if his wife knew then I thought of how funny it would be if I told her.

Bone and Run

by Elizabeth M. – Boulder, CO, age 23

When I was in college, I had my fair share of sorority and fraternity parties and games of tonsil hockey. Every year, the guy I deemed the hottest guy ever in a certain fraternity held a Christmas party. It was my duty to serve my sorority and women all over America by executing a stable plan: getting Bobby in his room, locking the door and having my way with him. Liquid confidence and perhaps my small figure yet huge set of gozongas had always helped me land these goals. It was the night of the party and I was pretty well sauced.

Of course, girls were flirting with Bobby and he loved the attention, so I had to up the ante. This obviously means, I hit the bathroom and pulled out my bronzer to really create that huge look of cleavage in my green tube top. Anyways, I decided to use the upstairs bathroom because it was conveniently closer to Bobby's room and he knew I was walking upstairs. At this point in my life, most guys knew that if I was walking upstairs towards their bedroom, I was a dead target for being the prime "sorostitute".

I walked out of the bathroom and to my happy surprise found him at his computer changing the rap song on his iTunes. I still do not understand why well groomed, white frat guys think that Biggie is their group anthem I never will know. Anyways, I walked in the room, made myself a comfortable seat on his lap and helped him pick out other tacky rap songs. My mind was clearly that I needed to execute the plan and I needed to do it quickly because there were Jello shots downstairs.

I switched positions, straddled him, felt Mr. Pokey in his pants and knew the time had come. I was going to land Bobby in bed. The more I write, the more I sound like a frat guy. Anyways, it was an unpleasant surprise when I tore off his comforter to find satin sheets. It gets worse, they were GOLD SATIN SHEETS. I was obviously loaded.

Regardless, I achieved my goal. I took advantage of Bobby and made sure he had me at the top of his booty call list. Then afterwards, Bobby said "I have a party to go check on I will be back". Weird, I thought. Wouldn't it just suck if he left me there? People walking in and out to change the music. Girls walking in looking for Bobby. I made myself a comfortable nest underneath his SATIN sheets and comforter so as to appear as a body shaped figure under his bed. No one could possibly catch on right?

I was nervous as hell to get up in my birthday suit. Lock the door and find my damn clothes. People were everywhere in that hallway. So I scrambled to the end of the bed to get my cell phone. I texted my friend Samantha: "Sam! Shit! I am in Bobby's room under his covers! I am the victim of a bone and run!" no response for a half hour. Finally Sam busts in and I had never been happier to see someone in my life. We could not find the pants I borrowed from a sorority sister that were not cheap or my right shoe anywhere. We looked literally all over his room, bed and closet. The plan was to get out of there ASAP though so it was time to run.

I threw on his very comfortable and what turned out to be his favorite pair, also most expensive of Nike sweats. I also threw on my left shoe. So I walked out of Bobby's room, into a crowd of acquaintances with my green tube top, Nike sweats and one black pump. Obviously my hair was a tangled mess in the back. As I walked down the stairs, I saw Bobby laughing and drinking with friends. WHAT-A-DICK.

Anyways I got out of there, trudged home in the snow with Sam and her boyfriend and was home safe. That week, the girl I borrowed the pants from was asking where they were. I said nowhere to be found but I will keep asking people to look. Between sorority pledges going on errands to find the pants and having his frat brothers try to find them we had no luck. She loved those pants.

Well the end of the year rolled around and the story obviously had not disappeared because as we packed up our rooms in the house, she said "can you just cut me a check for those pants Bobby stole?" so I did. And I am still convinced he has some strange fetish for a great pair of banana republic denim. Quite the happy holidays.

Fart

by Natalie R. – Chapel Hill, NC, age 36

I go with my sister to meet these guys with my sister. She is really in to one and I am just a back up. I was 18 and just realizing the fun of getting loaded and hooking up so when it turns out his friend is smoking hot and a little older than me which I love. I immediately order double vodka and set to charm him. We all go to a bar to dance and get better acquainted and by the midnight. I know this dude wants to get with me to so I check with my sister on her progress and she is ready to roll to so I say, "it is a shame we can not go somewhere else more intimate." My sister's date immediately suggests we go to his place with a built in bar and recreation room so we go.

My guy really admires how I can put away the booze and every time he looks at me I just know we have to be alone soon. They have a pool table and awesome stereo and I feel very sophisticated for some reason. We play pool and I make suggestive comments about balls and sticks but I was 18 and just feeling totally slutty around this guy.

However, my sister is sneaky and slinks off in to the adjacent bedroom first. As soon as we both realize they are gone I just attack him. Look and look for a more private spot but the only other room is a laundry room and where we are now. However, being young and extremely horny, we end up making out on the pool table and eventually were are naked and going at it. He was fantastic. However, even with the light off it is pretty hard to keep quiet so eventually we could hear my sister and her guys snickering behind the locked bedroom door.

This totally kills the mood so he picks me up and takes me in to the laundry room where in my desperate state it seemed just fine to go at it on a pile of dirty clothes. Vodka and hormones do that to you. By now the vodka is really taking effect and I am starting to regret drinking so much so fast but I am having a great time.

This guy has fantastic body and really knows what he is doing so that makes my head spin more. He whispers dirty talk in my ear and being 18 it sounds really hot and then he announces he is going to make me feel even better pulls out - NOOOOOO! And starts to work his way down my body with his mouth until he is between my legs.

By now, I am beyond drunk and can not get over how good this guy is and he is really gifted at oral sex unlike the guys my age. Suddenly he is shaking me saying "Natalie? Are you okay? Say something." Apparently too much vodka and advanced sexual skill was too much for me and I feel asleep. I apologize and say "God it was just so great". I felt like I was going to faint, did I? This seems to satisfy him and he goes back to it saying junk like "I could do this forever!"

Anyways I fall asleep again and when he wakes me again I let out a huge fart before he has a chance to move to safety and he is totally grossed out. "Oh gross! How could you do that?" and I said something dumb like, "um that was not me. I think something fell over in the corner". He says, "I do not think so. WOW that smells disgusting!" and starts to move away.

I was really embarrassed and frankly, bitchy because I just wanted to pass out now so I said, "the only thing that stinks here is this fucking laundry room, nice place you boys have!" and I hopped up to find clothes. It is really dark but as I am coming up to open the door I can hear his friend out in the recreation room laughing his ass off in the dark. He heard the whole episode and when I turn the door knob, he runs away to report the event to my sister. The next morning, neither one of the guys can look me in the eye and my sister and this insane grin on her face.

Seal the Deal

by Alyssa F. – Oakland, CA, age 23

The guy who took my virginity was a long time family friend that I occasionally hooked up with through out high school and college. When we finally did it, "seal the deal" his comment after we were done was. "I just had sex with my dad's best friend's daughter!" The expression and excitement was like "DUDE HIGH-FIVE!" I laughed at the time thinking it was pretty funny. That was the only time we ever had sex and he has my virginity to keep the damn bastard. I really thought and believed everything he had told me before that we were actually going to date, so that is why I didn't think much of it. Oh well I guess. But I am pretty for sure I was something to brag about with all his buddies. I hate men!

Three Boy Toys

by Patricia R. – Lubbock, TX, age 18

Up until this weekend, I had some pretty damn good hook up stories, most of which including my work and hooking up with both of my 28 year old bosses in various places while working in a pizza shop. Many lovely places in the shop including: the office, prep room, and my personal favorite, the walk in freezer. I was 18 and in high school at the time, and yes, both of them were married with children.

I am now a freshman in college experiencing the college lifestyle just a bit. So this past weekend, me and two of my good friends made a pact that we were going to get laid, neither of them have at school yet, but I had already made two booty calls from home. So Friday night we have just a tad of Grey Goose and went to my friend's dorm. He had a friend visiting from home just for the night. I set my eyes on him and decide that I am going to show him a great time here. We go to a party with a few friends and halfway through I grab him and we leave, go back to my room and to say the least, he spent the night in my room and it was very good but my story does not end there.

Saturday comes around, and everyone on my floor already knows and me helping out the new visitor, but I am not done yet for the weekend, this cougar is on the prowl. There was a huge highlighter marker party, just giving guys an excuse to write ridiculous things on girls, but we are not arguing it. I am there and once again before we got there we drank some Grey Goose of course, and we start dancing with everyone. This creeper gets behind me and he is grinding all up on me and so he is like lets go get something from upstairs, and shocking for me. I just say that I will wait for him on the dance floor, so as soon as he leaves this other guy comes and sticks his tongue down my throat, but my hot mess self decides to just go along with it. This leads to him and I in the bathroom, having sex on the sink, with a door that doesn't lock. Finally I end this mess of a situation and we need to get out of the bathroom before one more person in this party sees my vagina.

I go into another room of the party and get some of the gasoline jungle juice that the boys made aka wine, rum, and tequila. I end up seeing this boy who I always had a crush on and he calls me over we will call him hot pocket, he is pretty into me tonight so I am not argue. I go over and we are talking and low and behold, that kid from the bathroom followed me in there. Yes I do not know his name, so me and hot pocket escape from the party and go for a walk. Innocent? Yeah right. End up going back to his dorm room and I end up having sex with him twice and it was amazing drunken sex.

To say the least, this weekend was just a tad satisfying on my part, "doing the nasty" with three different guys, meeting two just this weekend, and not knowing one of there names still. It does not matter I will not see them again.

Fireworks

by Diana S. – Greene, NY, age 29

This is not so much a relationship story but more of a drunken hook-up. The guy involved did not dig the fact that I smoked in his bedroom so he would allow me but only if he had a candle lit. With only a candle for light we got busy and while in the midst of wild drunken monkey love my pillow shifted.

I thought holy fuck this is great. I really am seeing fireworks here. I have heard of it but never experienced it. Turns out that my pillow was on fire I tapped his shoulder and informed him. He was busy and without skipping a beat or breaking a stride he reached over patted it out on the floor and continued right along. Every time of think about it I feel so proud of him. That is really dedication to the sport.

Three Blind Mice

by Holly M. – AB, Canada, age 35

It is Halloween night somewhere back in the early 1990's and I am dressed as one of the three blind mice. I wore thick glasses and band aids on my ass where my tail had been cut off with a carving knife. I am at a Kim Mitchell concert in Red Deer, Alberta, Canada. I dragged along an ex boyfriend in case I ran out of money for drinks you should always part as friends and a younger female cousin of mine!

Well I am sure I don't need to tell you that The Kim Mitchell rocks a full house everywhere he goes. Provided they are hick town college gymnasiums so wcdgcd between my cousins the gorilla and a large set of grapes. That kept rubbing against me with that annoying balloon rubbing sound. The crowd is hopping to "I'm a wild party". Jammed in like a pack of wieners, sweating hot, fogging up my already hard to see through thick glasses. I feel a freaking hand between my legs rubbing up my peek-a-chu WTF? I can not see past the damn grapes better not be the gorilla. Cousins in these parts do not really role like that. The ex is somewhere doing a drink run so he would not have a spare hand so its there and its not there.

At just the right time I catch the hand and pulling it in and following it but am unable to catch a glimpse of the face it is attached to a grapes and glasses issue. I somehow hold on until the song wears down and the grapes back off a bit. I get this guy pulled off to the side and check him out only one in there not in costume and not all that attractive but male and of age.

Since I am drunk and it is Halloween long story short. Ditched the cousin and ex without even noticing and go off to fornicate on the shared living space floor of some yucky young guy's dorm room. Where I am sure I heard more people around and with my full make up and ears we get down and dirty.

Fast forward. I am done, half assed satisfied and now to find my group. Shit! Did not think to write down an address or number for my cousin's place and me and ex are from out of town. I did a lot of stumbling around looking like a drown rat not cute mouse until by some miracle they drove by and saw me. They are like "where did you go?" I said, "I was looking for you. Thanks for ditching me assholes!" They still do not know the whole story and have apologized repeatedly for losing me. I think that would have to be the years answer to the question. "Trick or treat?" This little trick was a treat.

Just as a side note. The really messed up thing is this guy I am living with now my boyfriend of two years from another town. He was the bouncer at that concert, just weird to have been in same place a decade ago although we never met that night. I am just thinking it must have been fate.

Dirty Green

by Misty H. – Albuquerque, NM, age 33

Back in 1992 I was 17 and pregnant, a girlfriend's younger brother who was 14 developed a crush on me. I told him when he turned 18 we could talk. He called me on his 18th birthday to let me know he was ready to talk. I laughed about it at the time. Flash forward to about 10 years ago.

I was visiting his sister at his house where he lived with his girlfriend at the time. He was away and we three girls got chatting. His sister, his girlfriend and I. We devised a plan to freak him out and play with him a bit since we all knew about the crush that he still carried for me. When he returned we were all sitting on front porch and left the only seat available for him right next to me on patio swing. When he sat down I moved a little closer. Everyone pretended not to notice, but he did. He kept looking to his girlfriend to see what she was thinking.

Then I started a series of questions to see how far I could take things. I said, "Hey, Jay what is you favorite color?" He says, "red?" I say, "what do you think of green?" "Green is ok I guess." I say, "Ok what do you think about dirty green?" "Dirty green?" I say, "Like my bra. As I lift my shirt to expose my green bra. "Do you think this is a dirty bra?" He looks at his girlfriends face while turning deep red. He says, "I guess I do like that color." I say, "But Jay, do you think this is a dirty bra?" In slutty and very dirty voice, he was squirming. He said nervously, "I do not know, I guess, what the f@*# are you guys up to?" We all just giggle and his girlfriend says, "come on Jay answer, do you like her dirty green bra?" He answered YES! So we teased him and played around like this for a while longer while getting really drunk.

Flash forward to later that night. Now it is time to head to bed, his girlfriend and I trade bras. Which she fills out much better than I did I must say. They head off into the bedroom and his sister and I can hear a lot of laughing and such. So we figure job well done and head to bed but that isn't where it ends.

My girlfriend and I get ourselves all tucked into a bed we are sharing in the basement and attempt to go to sleep. She falls asleep right away, but I am still awake. I hear footsteps down the stairs and over to her side of the bed. It is her brother he whispers, "are you awake?" I say, "she is sleeping Jay, what's up?" He comes over to my side and kneels down beside the bed, "are you sure she is asleep?" "Yes, she has been snoring for half an hour or more, she is asleep...why?"

"Well, my girlfriend and I were talking and she told me to come ask you if you were interested in joining us. She came up with it, so it is ok if you want to?" I was surprised. "What! Join you, like sex wise?" "Ya, it's up to you, of course I want you to. I am going to go back to bed come up if you want do not wake my sister up please." Sorry I know this story is dragging on but, it is such a long one!

After some careful drunken consideration I figure what the hell. Sure what do I have to lose and it was their idea. So I head upstairs and there they are waiting for me. HOW AWKWARD!

His girlfriend takes leader role and takes me hand leads me to their bed and undresses me. Instructs Jay to kiss me here and touch me there and what not. There we are in a full out three way deal. Sparing you guys all of the details in between. Jay and his girlfriend have this code, "Are you sure, OK" wink and nod conversation. She guides me by my hips onto him and I proceed to ride the poor boy. After the fun I ahead back to bed crawl in with the snoring girl, his sister. Next morning his sister and I wake up to an empty house. They are gone to work and no one is the wiser. Later in the day we all met up. HOW AWKWARD!

She proceeds to tell me that they had agreed ahead of time that there would be NO penetration between Jay and I. A small fact that was undeclared to me. But everyone is ok with the turn out and not

Chelsea Goldstein – www.chelseagoldstein.com

to worry. So I guess this is where my story ends. They are no longer together nothing to do with that night. No unwanted pregnancies or diseases, just a messed up three some.

This past July I was a bridesmaid at his sisters wedding. Her brother Jay was of course there and his ex girlfriend was also a guest. AWKWARD! His ex and I ended the night during the wedding by being the last two drunks on the dance floor. There is a happy ending to what most times could end up tragic. That is my one and only three adventure and although it all worked out and we are all friendly still. I do not recommend threesome. I would not attempt it again and God forbid my mother ever found out.

The Phone

by Brittney F. – Indianapolis, IN, age 19

I had been talking to this guy for a while meet him off the internet. I thought he was kind of cute or whatever so I seduced him over the phone and made him bike three miles one way to my apartment. We had not ever slept together before. I was not sure what to expect, and it was awful. He seemed to be a very confused little boy who did not know how to use his penis. He needed a instructional booklet. I was torn between laughing and crying for the 15 minute duration. I felt bad about how far he journeyed so I let him finish and then made him suit up and get the fuck out.

After he left I called an old friend whom I knew was capable in the bedroom and he came over. It is not fair that men can still have orgasms even when they suck in bed. If I can not, he should not either. But I guess I am too nice.

20 Year Old Virgin

by Leslie J. – Davenport, IL, age 20

I have a tendency to cause guys to cheat. My most current ex boyfriend cheated on three different girls. The one I knew about I just did not like her. She was a bitch to me. I did ask him if he was ok with her and of course he said yes. We had sex almost every day when he was with her or at least fooled around. Another girl and I also did not like her. She deserved it even more because she was my friend and decided she wanted to steal my boyfriend of two years. We had sex almost every day as well.

Normally in my car before school we would fool around. The third girl I did not know about and I was sort of friends with her so I felt a little feel bad. They only dated like two weeks so it was not really anything right? Guy number two, he cheated on two different girls with me. I was kind of fooling around with him. I found out he was dating someone at the time so we kind of stopped. Every time we talked or hanged out something would happen the joys of having a webcam.

While all of this was going on my ex's best friend was trying to get me to sleep with him. He is a 20 year old virgin. That is hard to find these days. I fool around with him a little when I had a threesome with him and my ex one night. He was the WORST EVER! Never again.

All of these things were going on at the same time. I have a pretty interesting sex life at time. Got a few guys. Possibly guys with a girlfriend that I may or may not know about the way I look at it is. I will be 20, so I am young and just having fun, completely safe, and clean. Plus when I meet the right guy I will have plenty of experience.

Get a Room

by Kelly H. – Wilmette, IL, age 20

My boyfriend and I parked in his aunt's driveway, which was also next door to his house. She was going to be working late so we parked next to a big storage so my car was completely hidden. We started hooking up in my car and for about 45 minutes we fooled around. When I finally put my seat up I looked in my mirror and saw his aunt getting out of her car. Three to four hours before I was told she would be home.

She parked about 10 feet away from my car and I have no idea how long she had been there or what she might have seen. I was so scared. His aunt seems conservative and really liked me. I did not want her knowing we were having sex. I had to drive past her to leave and she gave us a funny look almost like she was saying "you two get a room."

I was almost in tears because I did not want his family knowing either, we were only 18 at the time and I did not want his family thinking I corrupted their youngest son.

Life is Short

by Courtney B. – Norwalk, CT, age 27

A few years ago after breaking up with my first love, I became desperate for male attention and joined an online dating site called: American Sngles. One of the first guys I met name Chad. We exchanged pictures, talked for a few days and then he asked me out. He said he was in construction, 5'7" which is short for me and his picture he was sexy so I decided to give it a shot.

Chad picked me up in his sports car and he resembled Patrick Swayze. I noticed he was shorter than his profile suggested. So I thought to myself, I wore my shorter heels thank goodness. We get to the bar. He opens my car door like a perfect gentleman.

I realize he is 5'4". Standing there holding the door open. I am a petite busty woman he made me feel more like an AMAZON the whole date. He was telling me about all the women who have rejected him. I had to drink more just to pretend I was listening to him. I was thinking to myself when will this be over. This should have been a sign not to date online. So young and naive.

There was one thing he did that was smart. He kept on feeding me liquor. When I drink too much I became very horny and slutty. The more I drank I did not notice that he was so short. I ended up waking up naked at his house the next day at 2 p.m. in the afternoon. Needless to say, I went back on American Singles, drank too much, and met my loser ex boyfriend who knocked me up. That is a whole other story.

Birthday Present

by Alexandra P. – New Rochelle, NY, age 27

My best friend has a boyfriend who is a bartender for a popular lounge in New York City and Los Vegas with a huge penis. She only allows him to bring another girl, any girl he wants as a treat like on vacation or his birthday.

Last summer they chose me. I always thought he did not like me especially when I had a little crush. It turns out he asked her for months if we could all hook up they lived in a tiny studio apartment with perfect lighting for tripping, sex, and since he is also a DJ, he had a mix he created in the back ground.

It sounds like cheesy porn but with better drugs and much better music. They were two days ahead of me I had never done hard core drugs before I was 25 so the whole experience was amplified it felt so good. The touching, sucking, getting off ALL night long like a fantasy it kept going for hours, we lost track of time they were like my love gurus teaching me the ways to please a man and a woman. There were some added bonuses I do not know if you should know about. We even created a slogan "Peaches for Impeachment" because we hate George Bush.

Vampire

by Caitlin P. – Kissimmee, FL, age 25

It was my first date with my current boyfriend we got a hotel room at the beach. Because you know, nothing says awesome first date better than a hotel room prior to going anywhere. We could not find anywhere to go because we were in Brevard County, Florida which is like hicksville beach town. I know weird combination.

We drove around for hours looking for something to do and finally we found a strip-club in the middle of no where. There was like a Denny's across the street. I guess a Denny's across the street from anything makes the alternative seem like a better idea. So we decided to hang out at the strip club which was cleverly named, "Strip Club".

I had a 60-year-old stripper try to make out with me on the way in. And they're like playing 80's techno like freaking C and C music factory or some crap. And if that wasn't a red flag for me to leave, we decided to get a lap dance and apparently this strip club just appoints a random girl to you. You have no say in the matter. I mean as long as it was not Granny, I guess it did not really matter who it was. But it ended up being this stripper named Asia she was Asian. I wondered if there was a black stripper named Africa but that is beside the point.

This stripper looked 15, and she kept asking me how she should dance like she had never done it before so she moved side to side kind of like when 5 year olds try to dance to rap music and end up doing the twist. Then she tried to put her boobs in my face but her boobs were so small she had to grab them and pull them out. It looked kind of painful. She kept giving me this look like "Where am I?" and she tried to rub her ass in my date's face and his head pushed back. His drink knocked off the table half on me so he tried to reach down to pick it up but his hand touched a dead cockroach. Then the song that was playing started skipping and no one bothered to do anything about it. The stripper kept on dancing and she goes, "It always skips on this part". Eventually we finally gave her $20 bucks to stop.

On the way out the door granny was approaching, so we kind of ran out of there literally. We went to Denny's after that. Well we have been dating for three years now and my birthday is next month. So were thinking of going back there for my birthday and bringing my friends, since no one seems to believe us about this place. Maybe Asia will be of age by now. It kind of reminded me of From Dusk Till Dawn where the strip club ends up being Vampireville. Only I would have rather been hanging out with Quentin Tarantino's ugly ass, and been eaten alive by vampires.

Teamwork

by Kristin R. – Wilton Manors, FL, age 33

Back in college my roommate and I had a dirty three-some with the hot soccer player named Walter in our dorm room. We figured he was too hot for just one of us so we tagged teamed him for hours doing one unholy thing after another. So this went on for a few months until he transferred to Europe for a semester.

Fall came around, and all we had was some crazy memories. Then one night we saw him at a bar. He was visiting his very attractive friend Sam another guy on the soccer team. So we all go back to our apartment to hang out. We did not know who wanted who at that point so we all decided to get naked. I remember specifically Walter on his back while I was sitting on his face, while my roommate sucking his cock while getting it from behind from Sam all. After an hour or so we told them to leave I think we had boyfriends so they take off and we noticed Walter forgot his hat. We walked onto the balcony to yell and give him the hat. They were high fiving and hugging all the way down the block. All he heard was "I told you they were fun girls" we kept the hat and never saw them again.

Revenge

by Danielle L. – Royal Oak, MI, age 21

I was out at a bar one night, catching up with some friends at my old College. I was trying to get over an ex boyfriend who also went to that college and who was a long distance relationship. Some guys came over and bought my friends and me drinks, mind you this was after a drink was spilled all over my dress.

This one guy and I started talking and went back to his place to hang out. When I finally found out his full name, it was my ex's best friend that I never met since we were dating long distance. We hook up and did the nasty. When I was done we made drunken phone calls to him all night. It was the best revenge ever. Being beautiful gets you a lot apparently, and I loved that his best friend would betray him just because he got lucky.

Baby Bjorn

by Samantha H. – Macomb, IL, age 41

This past early August I went to Nevis with a girlfriend of mine as her guest since her husband could not go. She had to work event planner so I was mostly by myself at the pool. We stayed at The Ritz Carlton which is so not a ritzy there but still only the fancy people go there.

Every day at the pool I noticed this group of young guys in their twenties but I would just keep my shades on and my iPod and never spoke to them. I am married and 40 now I am 41 so what would they want with me anyways.

There is not a lot to do on Nevis but one night we went out to this little shack called Sunshine's. We started drinking of course and making eyes with one of the guys. Fucking HOT! Flirted and had fun but nothing happened.

Until. We are at the airport and from Nevis you have to fly to Florida and hang out for three hours until the next flight back home to Chicago. I see HOT boy alone reading. I nudge my friend to say, "Hey, hot boy's over there." She invites him to get a drink with us. He obliges and we sit at the bar for the three hours getting sloshed. I get very uninhibited and tell him right there that I would love to kiss his gorgeous young baby face.

His name was Bjorn by the way so in order to keep it straight I kept referring to him as "Baby Bjorn". He takes my hand and asks me to walk with him. So, smiling and winking at my girlfriend, I go. I was so nervous and excited because I had a feeling something was going to happen but I have not even kissed another guy since I met my husband 9 years ago. I felt more excited over Baby Bjorn and I think I might have peed in my pants or something.

We went around the corner and totally made out and felt each other up and down in a corner at the airport. I am sure everyone was looking at us but I did not care because I figured nobody would ever see me or him or we would see each other ever again. Until I got on the plane and everyone was staring at me and every once in a while making a moaning noise I know was directed at me. Oh well it was hot and juicy and nobody but my girlfriend, Baby Bjorn, and now you know this and Miami's entire airport.

We did not exchange any info it was a one time only thing. He rocked my world for a little while. Then I felt guilty but I am going to the grave with it because my husband would be so pist off if he ever knew. Married life is not so juicy to kiss and tell.

Subway Ticket

by Alicia C. – San Fransisco, CA, age 19

When I was 16 I was hanging out with my friend mike and his friend whose name is completely lost to me. We were in a van and I was out of money and needed to take the Bay Area equivalent of the subway home. The guys said they had a ticket they didn't need but they wanted to know what they would get in return.

They asked me to go down on them and I said fine because I was going through a phase where I did not really give a fuck what I put in my mouth. They pulled the van over and I spent like five minutes with the smallest penis I had ever seen in my mouth until then next guy's turn. Seriously they were each smaller than my thumb! And it turned out that the ticket they gave me had no money on it. So I had to call my dad to pick me up. I have spent three years trying to forget that afternoon.

Buddy

by Katrina J. – McKinney, TX, age 19

I spent three weeks in Denver at a summer study type camp and I became close to this girl named Jasmine. We were hanging out one night smoking cigarettes when we met these three older guys. Jasmine had a boyfriend at the time so she tried to set me up with the hotter of the two who did not seem to be gay. We exchanged numbers but he kept asking me to set him up with Jasmine.

I tell her how I have been shot down and she decides to take a break from her boyfriend and start seeing buddy. I swear to God that is the guy's real name. However, Jasmine is not brave enough to spend time with Buddy solo, so I tag along. Well, it seems that buddy is not all that brave either, so he brings along his friend Chad and the two of us hit it off pretty well.

After talking over the phone for like 18 hours, Chad and I finally get the chance to get it on, and the sex is ok but nothing to write home about. Two days go by and Jasmine and Buddy break up. Jasmine tells me she wants to get back at Buddy for leading her on. He sent her a picture of his dick or a dick, that's 10 inches long, but never, delivered the goods.

Anyway, I am still three days away from leaving Denver and decide I need one more fuck for the road. So I give Chad a call and tell Jasmine that I figured out how she could get back at Buddy by having a threesome with me and Chad. She's down with and so is Chad. The sex with him was better that time but it may have had something to do with the fact that there was someone else in the bed, and she knew where the clitoris is and how it functioned. The funniest part of the story is that my sister was in Denver with us but she never knew why I kept hanging out with Chad and his "Buddy."

Fights

by Cassandra C. – Dayton, IN, age 20

I dated this guy and he was a huge badass well at least thought he was. He was training to be a UFC fighter, but was like only 5'7" but then I was thinking that sometimes short guys are packing a lot in the pants but when we finally did it. Which was abut 5 hours after we met he was hung about as much as my 3 year old neighbor. It was very unsatisfying and he ended up cheating on me with his ex who was 6'1" which is ridiculous. I dumped him and told him how his dick was nothing to write home about and he was like, "Well bitch you never complained!" and I did not even know what to say to that because he already has so much going for him what with the UFC fighting and the small dick. I felt like taking the high road and ignore him, but it was funny.

One Ball

by Amy H. – Encino, CA, age 20

One time at school I was trying to have a one nighter with this kid who unfortunately had a crush on me which not happening. Since I have not had sex in a while so I was like why not and even though he smelled like he was a bottle of cheap tequila. He came in less than three minutes. I was like you have to be kidding me and I was pissed and he had the balls to ask me how he thought it was. At least someone came because I sure as hell did not and he left.

Just last night my boyfriend and I were fooling around and I went to grab his dick. I panicked because as I was stroking I thought I only felt one ball. I got really freaked out because I dated a guy with only one ball. He was a pussy and would not ever let me make jokes about or call him UNO.

I did not want to deal with all that again so then I was grabbing his balls which he either enjoyed or thought was equally as awkward as I did.

Chelsea Goldstein – www.chelseagoldstein.com

Thankfully found his other one which was hiding I did not know they could separate like that I thought they pretty much stuck together but I was incredibly relieved.

Crabs

by Sarah C. – Irvine, CA, age 23

Once upon a time my friend Alisha was a struggling actress in Los Angeles. She was working as a dental assistant in Century City and fantasized about being a famous actress.

Her first brush with fame happened in spring 1971. As Alisha got hired to house sit the house of a famous TV star of the 1970s. The fabulous house was conveniently located in the Hollywood hills. Making it easy for Alisha to discover the Hollywood scene. She could not believe she was getting paid to do this. The actress would call weekly to make sure the house and Alisha were ok. What an easy job.

Now, you have to understand that my friend Alisha is a good Jewish girl. She goes to temple every week and hides her JNF blue box under her bed. She is the boring kind of friend even today at 60 years old. But I keep her around as a friend so she can be my designated driver.

One morning, Alisha felt an itch down there. She

got a little worried. A few hours later it became really itchy and she felt compelled to scratch in public. She could not take it anymore and ran to her OB-GYN.

That is when he broke the news to her "Sorry you have got crabs!" "Crabs" she screamed! "How did that happen?" she asked. "Well you know they can be found everywhere really," the doctor replied.

The next morning when the actress called the house, Alisha told her what she going through and asked if by any chance she knew if there was a possibility she could have gotten them at the house.

The actress paused and admitted to Alisha that she had had crabs herself a few months ago. "How did you forget to tell me that there were crabs in your sheets?" Alisha screamed.

"Well I don't know, I thought they would be gone by now" the actress said. "I am going to have to leave, find yourself a new house sitter!" she replied. After a pause started laughing and said. "Well if it is any consolation they were Ringo Starr's!"

Hollywood

by Brittany C. – Woodbury Heights, NJ, age 20

I decided we were going to come out to Los Angeles and go all out. We wanted to have a one night stand. It was my first time out on the west coast and me and my friend decided to go to a Dodgers and Phillies game. We live right near Philadelphia and follow the team so it was perfect that they were out there the same time we were.

At the game we met a bunch of guys. They were all Mexican and were hitting on me and my friend really bad. We decided to sit with them and ended up having a great time. This was a plus because the next night they called us and wanted to take us out for a night in Hollywood. We agreed. And were both hoping that we would get to fulfill our dreams of one night stands.

After a couple shots of Grey Goose and a night at the Saddle Ranch Bar in Hollywood we went back to our hotel. Me and one of the Mexican guys started to make out in my room and it was going okay until he started to dry hump me. Normally I would not mind this but he did not know he was humping the inside of my thigh. This went on for a few minutes. I was hoping he would move his junk over and it did not happen. He kept saying "How does it feel baby?" "Does it feel good?" and I did not know what to say. I was starring at the ceiling praying he would stop or change positions.

I told him "oh it is so good" and tried to move around under him to rearrange it for him. Now during this whole time he was trying to be sexy and lick me I guess. My face and neck were soaked with this guys spit. It was not very attractive. Finally I told him I was not into this and got up and went in the other room where my friend was, and asked her if we could kick the guys out. She said no.

I was still drunk, so when my friend told me to go back into the room I did. By the time I got back into the room luckily he was passed out, so I crawled back into bed hoping not to wake him and I passed out too. The next morning was horrible. The two guys we brought back did NOT want to leave. We told them we were getting ready and dropped numerous hints that it was time for them to leave.

They ended up coming to breakfast with us and finally leaving after we started saying we were going out for the day. The thing that really upset me was I was really hoping to get a little action in bed before I had to go back to reality in New Jersey and unfortunately the only thing that got action was my leg and his penis.

Naked Girl

by Lindsay T. – Glendale, NY, age 21

Went out to a keg party one night with some friends and had several drinks. The party was, as expected, broken up by the cops early, and I ended up going downtown to a club with three guys I had just met at the party, whose names I could not seem to recall. The club we went to usually lets mostly girls in, so I ended up going in by myself as they waited in line.

Wandering into the bar, completely drunk, I decide to get myself a drink as I am by myself and do not know who is there. After getting my drink, some fellow with red hair starts talking to me. For some reason, he asks me, if you had to sleep with any guy here right now, not including me, who would you choose? I scan the crowd, and describe a sexy brunette guy in a graphic tee chilling at the bar with some friends. I ask him the same question, he chose some girl whom I cannot describe because everything was a blur. I tell him good choice, then I come up with a great plan: let both go hit on them!

I go up to sexy buddy in the graphic tee and asked him to dance with me, and then drag him to the dance floor. We dance for a few songs, he is super hot up close and eventually he asks me if I want to go get a drink, to which I respond, and Can we just go back to your place? He appears a little taken aback, but not much later we were outside, I hailed a cab, and soon we were at his apartment building hooking up in the elevator.

It was very hot and getting just slightly explicit until some other dude came in, apologizes for interrupting, and then we continue up the elevator until we get to what I can only assume was his place. We hook up on the couch, things are going great, and then I ask him to get a condom. I am extremely turned on, and have been really enjoying what he has been doing to me and am pretty excited for what is to come.

Then the night takes a turn for the worst as this guy is unable to maintain an erection. He tried for a while and him getting it in for a bit and then prematurely ejaculating. That seems a bit contradictory if you ask me. And then getting hard again if you can call it that and trying a bit more we eventually give up and I pass out on the couch half naked.

His friends come in ask who the naked girl on the couch is he covers me with a blanket I get dressed and try to leave without confrontation but he follows me out and walks me outside, etc. The next day I receive a text from an unknown number that says, Hey remember me? I respond with, I do not know this number but I am assuming this is Alex the guy that I hooked up with. He writes back with, who is Alex? This is Chris. We have been talking a little bit since, it turns out his name is Chris. I have seen him since as well. It turns out he is just as hot as I remembered, but I have not had a chance since to see if he is capable of any follow through.

Seamen

by Casey J. – Marietta, GA, age 30

Eons ago my best buddy at the time and I really loved going out to one particular local club to dance. We were 18 year old virgins then, and we ended up picking up a group of Seaman. Boy, were they completely unlucky befriending the two virgins in the room.

So the next weekend I ended up bringing home three of these guys my parents were out of town and of course they bought us wine coolers. Which could have turned into a horrible situation but it was cool.

At some point each and everyone of them ended up completely stark raving naked and in my pool. Of course, I was a completely freak out and did not join them what a NERD! Remember I was a virgin at the time. Eventually I took the hotter one back to my bedroom and gave him a blowjob. And let me tell you, I have never had a bigger dick in my mouth since that night. In fact, the next lucky guy I blew was such a Eric, Mr. Big Cock from Houston, here is to you!

His Friends

by Victoria C. – Fairfield, OH, age 25

I was dating this guy back in February. He was a really really good guy. One night I got mad at him because he said he was tired and I ended up going to a bar with one of his friends. I started venting to his friend about being angry with him, and then I took his friend home with me and ended up sleeping with him.

He never found out about that. A week later, he got mad at me for showing up a half hour late drunk to go to a movie with him. Whatever, he really wanted to see Jumper and I knew in order to sit through that, I needed a little help from my friend vodka. So we went to the movie and our date ended early that night. I ended up bumping into a mutual friend of ours, who was not aware that we were dating and I ended up bringing him back to my place and hooking up with him, too.

The guy I was dating must have found out about that one because he never asked me to go out on a date with him again. I guess I would not want to go out on a date with him again if he slept with two of my friends within six days of each other while we were dating. We were never really a couple, so, it is really not that bad, right?

What's That Stain?

by Latoya G. – Fort Wayne, IN, age 25

There was a guy in my life that I barely know, but I am super attracted to him. Well, he is not really in my life, but he really wants to infiltrate, if you know what I mean. Penetrate!

This guy and I have never had a conversation that lasted more than five minutes. We exchanged numbers recently and we have this weird, racy text message exchange thing going on. He wants to take me to one of those seedy rent-by-the-hour motels. Is it crazy that I'm really considering doing it? I am dying of curiosity what the room looks like. I want to play "what's that stain" or "what's that smell". The game varies depending upon how recently the room was previously used. I hope the room has a TV equipped with HBO because I need to catch up on Entourage.

Sebring

by Sara K. – Springfield, MO, age 22

After my graduation from high school my friends and I went to a graduation party at a friend of ours trailer out in the middle of the woods. It was more like a run down Winnebago but whatever, so this other senior guy, Jake, was there with his bitchy junior girlfriend, Kelly. That I hated, so I thought, why don't I try to hook up him since we fooled around all during high school.

My friends told me that in a few weeks Jake would be leaving to go to Europe for the summer and if I did not make my move tonight that I probably would not get another chance to get it on with him and piss off his ugly ass girlfriend Kelly. I got wasted from Sky vodka and cranberry juice and made my move. I got Jake away from that bitch, which by the way was no easy task. I had to distract her with talking about cheerleading and once I got on her good side, I asked her to go get me a drink. Then I went to steal her man.

We headed straight for the trailer when I realized that there was only one bed room and two other couples were already using it and I am pretty sure that if one more couple would have been anywhere in there it would have fallen on its side. I went to plan B, my best friends 1999 two door Chrysler Sebring. We somehow managed to get into the back seat and get the bottom portion of our clothes off and steamed up the back seat.

When we were finished I wrote on the back window on the steam I just fucked your boyfriend in hopes that his girlfriend would see and to my surprise she did, I did not know her dumbass could read. She confronted him about it when he stepped foot out of the car. I gladly got out and explain myself to her in terms she could understand. She immediately broke up with him and left the party with some other cheerleaders and then Jake and I then decided that we should go for round two.

After that we then proceeded to sleep in the car. I slept on the steering wheel until the next morning when I was greeted by my friend who owned the Sebring. She was super pissed because I got her car dirty with his sperm all over the back seat of her car. I was really happy that I pissed Kelly off and got it on with Jake.

Knoxville

by Sarah B. – Las Vegas, NV, age 22

One night I was going out with some of my girls and we had started out at some bars. Than I realized I was out of money, so we went to the nearest ATM. I walked up and there was this hot guy there so after he got his 300 bucks out. I flirted with him and he ended up going with me and my friends to a house party where I then learned he was from Knoxville Tennessee.

So one thing led to the other and we got it on at the house party and needless to say when I exited the room all of my girlfriends were standing there looking at me. They all started chanting the word Knoxville to mc thcy still call me that to this day. So my hookup story is all about locations where you can meet a F*ckable guy, just about anywhere. I do not limit myself to bars. ATM's are just as good. I still do not know the guys name.

Dog Cage

by Dana P. – North Andover, MA, age 21

My friends and I were having a house party and kegger to celebrate the end of summer. There were a ton of people in the two story house and it was mass chaos with keg stands, beer bongs, and countless shots. Now when I get drunk and after getting flipped right side up after numerous keg stands. I can not think with my mind because the blood rushes from my brain to my vagina aka Betsy. I named her when I was eight years old. This was also the same time when my boobs were named Scruff and McGruff.

By about 11:00 p.m., I was on my 8th or 9th-ish beer, so it was time for business regardless of the amount of drunken strangers wandering throughout the house. There was one close guy friend I had in mind at this particular moment so, Betsy and I, with condoms in hand stumbled upstairs, through the first and second floor, and into the attic in search of my friend, Richard.

To mine and Betsy's surprise I found him tied up with a dog leash being lead into the dog's cage by two random girls. Thankfully, the dog was nowhere in sight. I said to him once I saw the freak show, so I hope you created a safe word. He chuckled and said were just having fun right ladies? One of the girls, I recognized as my lab partner. The other had a ladle filled with bottle caps and was attempting to feed Richard the bottle caps, weird.

Why he would allow them to do this, I didn't know. Until I remembered he is a male. My other drunken friends were also upstairs witnessing the events. Sam, who was sitting on a couch directly next to the dog cage and Daryl, who was on the floor in front of the couch placement, becomes key as the story advances.

The two boys were in uncontrollable laughter at how excited Richard was being tied up and all in the hopes of getting laid. I will give it to the two girls that they were good looking. I am pretty sure an actual locomotive could have been run through the both of them considering some of the stories my lab partner had told me.

Anyways the next thirty seconds happened very quickly. I sat on the couch to watch the show when suddenly the lights went off. I heard the two girls beat ass down the attic stairs giggling like morons. Immediately after the lights went off, I felt a hand go down my pants and another one was nudging on my side. This was not the odd part because I recognized the hands as my former lover Sam's soft girly man hands. As soon as I felt the hand down my pants, I had another one go up my shirt followed by another. These hands were rougher and I was not drunk enough to think that Sam's was that talented or capable of sprouting extremities. To top it off, I felt two more hands rubbing on my calf and up my thigh. I knew that Daryl was on the floor next to me. He had already been with one of my best friends earlier in the night, so I kicked him hard enough to let him know I was not interested in sloppy seconds.

The grip on my thigh was released and I heard him lumber down the attic stairs. In the meanwhile, there was a crisscrossing of hands occurring over my abdominals. I kept thinking do they know the other is there? Because I would make out with one and then switch to the other.

Finally, Richard asked me who was else was involved in the menagerie. I thought quickly not wanting the potential threesome to end because of my newly raised pimp status and I told him that Sam was one of the two girls. Considering Sam's hands were softer than a puppy, he bought it. After what seemed like hours, which ended up being only a few minutes, my threesome was stopped by my best friend turning the attic lights on and hollering up the stairs, Hey Skankbait! Put your clothes on were doing shots! I pulled my pants up and took my shirt down over my head that had been wrapped around my head like my grandmas babushka.

I was too drunk to fully take all of my clothes successfully off due to my shoes and my massive amount of humidity induced Rosanne Rosannadanna hair. As I was fumbling down the stairs I saw my best friend and realized she had no idea how accurate her previous statement had been. Of course, my threesome became a secret between me and everyone else at the party.

Later that night after the shots commenced, my whorish acts picked up and I proceeded to make out with my lab partners extremely cute boyfriend followed by his best friend since grade school. She still has no idea and if she did know I doubt I'd be typing this right now. That night has been one I've not been able to live down.

Chode

by Karen P. – Westport, CT, age 19

I have an odd hookup story that happened couple of years ago which I am still kind of like uncertain what the fuck happened. I am 19 and am going to be a sophomore in college.

There was this kid Anthony in high school that I had a huge crush on for a few years. He was very cute he was the captain of the lacrosse team, was like 6 ft. tall, and had wavy brown hair. He graduated the year ahead of me so he was in college and was home for the summer. He was the kind of kid that you would just want to fool around with he would be a horrible boyfriend.

We were at a party and everyone was drunk, so he asked me to go upstairs with him, cliché. We started fooling around, and when I was about to unzip his jeans he kind of freaked out. I remember him stopping me and being like "hold on a second" and he kind of ran to the bathroom. I waited a couple of minutes and seeing as I was drunk and horny, I got extremely frustrated. So I went to the bathroom to see what the hell he was doing. I knocked and there was no answer. I knocked again no answer. So I checked to see if it was locked and it wasn't so I just walked in. Anthony was standing with his back to me flogging his log. I just stood there for a second in shock. I clearly would have done it for him. I did not know what this meant? Was he like phobic of girls touching his dick? Did he have some sort of problem? He heard me come in a second late and turned around.

What I saw scarred me to this day. For a guy who was an athlete, I was expecting a normal sized member. What I saw was a knob. I am not talking about when you hear girls say he has a chode to be bitchy. In the biological sense of the male form, this guy had a chode. It was about two and half inches long hard. It must have gone the other way when it was soft. When he turned around I looked at it and I do not even remember how I reacted. I must have either screamed or said something really offensive, because Anthony turned really red and called me a "fucking insensitive whore" and left the party.

I was pretty insulted, he called me insensitive. He started up with me and left me on the bed. I have only seen Anthony once since. I was doing a run after working out and I looked pretty disgusting. I saw him paying for something and I caught his eye for a second and he gave me a death stare and stormed out. None of my friends know I feel too bad ruining his reputation. Whenever they say he is cute or mention anything about him at all I get very uncomfortable.

Chelsea Goldstein – www.chelseagoldstein.com

Junior Varsity

by Jacqueline B. – Glenhead, NY, age 19

To be very honest with you, I never saw myself as a slut. I lost my v-card when I was 17 and it was to a boyfriend that I had for a year. I am what people call a junior varsity slut. I hook up with random guys but do not let them go all the way. I heard this term recently and I think it is hilarious.

Here is my story. I was at a party and I was pretty intoxicated having played and won 8 games of beer pong mixed with Franzia wine chugs. The result was my having sex with this kid in the pool. It was not a stranger as I have hooked up with this guy drunkenly over the past several years. The slutty thing about it is that at the time, there were a bunch of people in the pool who were extremely focused on a game of beer pong on a floatable beer pong table. I did not think any of them knew what was going on, and I was too drunk to care. It was awesome I have never done it in a pool before and I really enjoyed myself.

Later that night I conked out on a couch in the basement. As I was falling asleep, I was awoken by someone sticking their tongue in my mouth in a dart like fashion. I opened my eyes a little to get a glimpse of who it was and it was someone I have never seen before. I do not even remember seeing him at the party at all. I got scared and I just kept pretending I was sleeping to see if he would stop. The horn dog sincerely thought I was passed out and felt me up, and started to go down to my happy place.

At that point, pushed him off me and asked him what the fuck was wrong with him. He told me he saw me sexing in the pool and that I was hot. I found this kind of odd and twisted that he would secretly watch me have sex, then pursue me the same night. Actually I was pretty shocked he pursued me at all after seeing me do that. I did not even know what to say, so he did most of the talking. As it turns out, he was gorgeous and goes to school somewhere in the Midwest. I figured I will never see him again. So I let him eat me out and for me that was a pretty slutty night.

Silvia and Steve

by Lindsey P. – Huntingon Beach, CA, age 21

One time I had a small party at my house which included a couple of my friends, my cousin, and a few of her friends. A lot of drinking ensued, of course, and eventually I passed out on my couch. I was awoken at around 4 a.m. by this girl Silvia and her boyfriend. I can not remember his name, we will call him Steve. Silvia and Steve were friends with my cousin. No one else was there and I was a little confused, and still very drunk. They were also very drunk.

Silvia looks at me and says "My boyfriend thinks you are hot, and I must agree. Do you want to mess around?" So okay, I am 18 years old at this point and so drunk I could not even speak properly so of course I said "OK!"

We are all making out and then clothes start to come off. I suggest moving to my bedroom. We make it to the bed, we are all ass naked now. Too drunk to function, and sloppily trying to pleasure each other. This goes on for about an hour until Silvia starts paying more attention to me than her boyfriend. Steve is starting to get pissed off. He removes himself from the snarled mess of arms and legs and Silvia and I keep on keeping on. Eventually, Steve gets so mad that he jumps off the bed and starts screaming at us. He runs out the front door, ass naked, and gets in his car and leaves.

Silvia starts crying saying, "oh my God, oh my God, he is going to break up with me oh my God," and I don't have the slightest idea what to do or say. So I am just sitting there, I grab a shirt and shorts from off my floor and get dressed. Meanwhile, Silvia can not find her shirt or her bra. My room was a huge mess of dirty laundry to begin with, so I could see why she was having trouble.

I walk into my living room and sit in the chair. Completely bewildered by what was going on. Suddenly, Silvia without her shirt comes into the living room and sits in my lap and starts making out with me hardcore. Then Steve fucking walks back into my house, right as this was happening and World War Three beings again. Lots of arguing and screaming ensue, he is calling her a dyke, she is telling him his dick is too small, etc. I am still sitting there clueless as to what to do.

Finally, they get their heads on straight and leave. He is still naked and her still topless. I go to bed. The next day, Silvia calls me and says "Hey, sorry about last night. We do not normally do things like that. I would appreciate it if you did not tell your cousin, and would it be okay for us to stop by and get the rest of our beer?" I was like, "sure?" But they never came. I did not see either of them for a long time until our mutual friend, my cousin, had her high school graduation party about six months later. It was awkward, to say the least.

Smiler

by Anna S. – Boston, MA, age 23

I was a pretty enormous slut. Back when I was visiting colleges that I wanted to play soccer at, I was invited to Johns Hopkins. Even though I knew JHU was really way out of my league mentally, I figured I would still go seeing as it was a prime excuse to party and hookup. Unfortunately for me, I was housed with a huge prude loser we will call her SMILER.

She sucked, and when she brought me to a basketball game, I had to take it upon myself to make some new friends, and find male soccer players for potential hookups for the night. Lucky me I aligned myself with a player that was having a party that night. I had to practically beg SMILER to let me go, obviously she said no but thank God her roommate said yes and brought me there. After several Lemonade Vodka concoctions someone else had made me I was pretty sure I had been roofied and would not need to break out my flask.

Shortly after my drinks I found myself in a room

with the captain of the team giving him head. I do not understand how I came to that, but I did. I do however recall the door not being shut and SMILER's roommate seeing what I was doing. I was not about to stop just cause she saw I did not think it would be fair to anyone. I already engaged myself in this task and this was the guy that invited me to the party so I figured I owed him at least that.

After that interaction SMILER'S roommate was disgusted with my actions and said she was going home, and I told her it was about time and that I had find my way back to her dorm at a more appropriate hour after 3 a.m. My hookup disappeared I wish I could give him a name but I never got it, so I moved on to a different party where I continued to slam shots.

I met a new guy from the soccer team who I made out with obscenely in public which when I think back to it now I really wish I would have found his room earlier and spared everyone else at the party that display. Once we made it to his room we hopped on his bunk bed and got to business. He was having some problems getting hard I think or hmm my memory really is not what it used to be after the amount of black outs I had but, I believe there was some sort of problem that resulted in a limp dick between my legs. Who knew his drinking was going to lead to this sad display so we made out for a little longer and I said my friend was leaving and I had to go which really meant I needed to find someone more proficient. I found someone who in my mind was cuter, and was hard already so I knew I would not run into the same problem. He said we could go to his apartment and that it was right around the corner.

Thirty minutes and seriously blistered feet later, we arrived at his smelly apartment. Thank God he had some vodka because after the walk I was starting to question this hookup. A couple of shots later we bounced on his bed and finally I was ready for some penetration. Hook up number three again I had no idea what his name was wanted to do something else like jerk off between my boobs. I was really thrown when this started to occur and I needed to exit immediately. He was pretty forceful so I had to sit back and wait. It was really gross to have to wipe cum off my chest but I did it with one of his t-shirts I found on the floor and instantly felt better about what has just occurred. I grabbed one of his sweatshirts and when he was in the bathroom bolted.

I am from NYC and I was all alone in Baltimore which is pretty scary. It was freezing out and as I was running back in the direction I thought I came in, I saw the first guy I blew on the street and when I got closer. I asked him how to get back to the dorms or at least to his house, but I became more positive that it was just a look a like and not him at all when he was blonde and I think my guy had brown hair but I am sure at that point in the night me determining hair color was far gone.

I was pretty abandoned with some holes in my jeans from falling down and I accepted it was time to call SMILER. She was not happy and I told her that her roommate left me she had to come get me. And the next thing I remember is leaving in the am. I did get many phone calls after that night one from SMILER'S roommate's boyfriend who I had phone sex with a few weeks later. Apparently I was pimping myself out to future hookups in the event I returned in the fall to attend school which I did not I was actually not allowed. When the coach called me on Monday to tell me that there was some negative feedback from the girls I really wondered what he was talking about.

Donkey Kong

by Kelsey B. – Bismarck, ND, age 20

It was a warm summer evening and I had two options. Attend a party full of people I only moderately tolerate or spend the evening with the Nintendo 64, which I recently rescued from my parents basement. Since Donkey Kong and his little monkey sidekick had been kicking my ass in multiple rounds of Mario Kart, I opted for the party.

Upon arriving I noticed my liquor choices were limited and stupidly decided it was an Everclear kind of evening. Forsaking my normal vodka or rum cocktail for a large glass of what can only be described as gang bang in a bottle is about the last thing I remember. Cut to 12 hours later, me waking up on my friends couch in a t-shirt promoting a football team I do not support. Because I do not support any football teams, I realized this was not my shirt. Possibly a little too full of my self, I crept out of the apartment and drove home, mocking the other hot messes still passed out on the floor.

A couple of hours later, thinking my dignity remained in tact, I got online hoping to ask one of my friends what had transpired the night before. Unfortunately, I did not have to. I opened my face-book account to find a link sent to me in a message. It was a Youtube video of me from the previous evening, making out with one of my girlfriends and then launching into a rousing rendition of what I embarrassingly admit was a number from Rent.

Talk about reliving your blackouts. I thought that was only supposed to happen when you dropped acid. To top it off, the video ended with a remark about Ruben Studdard and grape Kool Aid that certainly was not fit for the public space. It took a lot of begging for my friend to take my drunken escapades off the internet. Hopefully he will not realize that bottle of vodka I gave him as a bribe is actually half Aquafina.

Penguin

by Lisa W. – Woodhaven, MI, age 20

I did hookup with a guy in a penguin costume while dressed as a Smurf. We somehow managed to fool around with him still in the costume and then when the time came to fully unzip it and take it off. Imagine a large padded costume we discovered he was stuck. The zipper stopped just above his crotch. He then suggested I climb in the costume with him, which after several drinks seemed like the logical thing to do. His beak kept hitting my forehead, an attempt to change positions resulted in a two story bunk bed fall, and we had to cut ourselves free. I have not been able to look at penguins the same way since.

Twins

by Christine P. – Grayslake, IL, age 21

There was this really shameful incident on Cinco De Mayo. Atrociously shameful in fact, this boy name Roger and I were physics lab partners and decided a Cinco De Mayo party at Shady's Mojito Lounge was the perfect opportunity to take it to the next level. Normally I am not a fan of PDA, but it was 50 cent Jello shot night, so any shred of class I normally exhibit was lost.

We start really going at in an empty private room we luckily found in the back when he realizes we need condoms. As he sprints to CVS drug store, I venture out into the main area for another drink while I wait. I soon see Roger, run up and start making out with him and pulling him to the back room. He seemed a bit more shy than before, but he totally went with it. Soon we are both naked and right as I ask where the condoms are. The real Roger walks in, holding a box of Trojans and a cowboy hat.

Turns out the penis I was holding belonged to his

twin brother Evan. "You never told me you had a twin!" I slurred and shouted as I glared at both of them. As an intensive shouting and gesturing match escalated between the brothers, I threw on my dress backwards, grabbed my friend Jill and a couple more jello shots, and fled the premises. Next week I found out Roger had switched to another physics class. I do not know why but I have a lingering suspicion it was my fault.

Hamster

by Valerie L. – Southington, CT, age 21

You are in the middle of a drunken make out. Wait take that back a wasted and sloppy make-out session. You barely know what is going on. What you do know though is that at this point, you have no shame. If this make-out session continues to progress at this rate, the clothes are coming off. Mindless of the fact that you are in the middle of a party. Hopefully, if you picked the right partner for the night's festivities, that person is in the exact same boat and neither one of you will hold each other back.

Just clear sailing towards terribly embarrassing and stupid decisions. Luckily for me though, I have great friends that know me so well that just as I and the boy I am with is making the crossover from PG-13 to R-rated actions. They steer me in the direction of some privacy.

Whether this is finding a tree large enough so that some people will not completely know what is going on back there or simply throwing me in the shower and making sure the shower curtain is closed. I know I can always count on my friends to help me when I am ready to make some bad decisions. With a combination of my absent decision making skills, and my love for attention and facebook photos. It is best that I perform my wild actions away from people who may possibly have cameras accessible. So, really thank God my friends have learned to acquire that skill.

Anyways, it is going exactly as I said. Drunk me, drunk guy, making out, my friend points me in the direction of the basement. Now, I have been in this basement plenty of times before, and what I know from past experiences is that there is a couch down there. JACKPOT.

Life could not be better. With a little help from my friend this potentially disastrous situation has almost turned out to be completely acceptable. We waste no time and go strait to the couch. Then, yes it happens probably within seconds of being down there, we have sex and everything is going well. Keep in mind though as you read this just exactly how drunk I said the two of us were.

Next thing you know the guy I am with tells me he has to pee. What the hell did he want from me a hall pass to the bathroom? Ok, cool go ahead. I guess I misunderstood though. He was trying to figure out where to go to the bathroom. Well, the only one that I knew of was upstairs, which seemed like a hike to me. That not only consisted of heading all the way back up to a party of people, but that would also mean putting clothes back on, and possibly waiting in line for a bathroom that at this point, God knows how many drunk girls who can't handle their alcohol are throwing up in. The only response that came out of my mouth at this point was that sucks. But, I guess I am not the only person in town with drunken brilliance. He points out to me a hamster cage that is only a few feet away. Go for it I told him, it wasn't like I cared or would even remember something like that in the morning. Bedtime.

So I do not think much about this night as I wake up the next day. Honestly, at this point I would have told you it was one of my few successful nights. Time goes on and still do not give much thought to that night, not until a conversation I have one day in high school. I was in high school at this point with the kid whose house we were at. To my surprise, that perfect spot in the basement on the couch that I thought I was so lucky to find, was surrounded by my friend's middle school sister and her friends having a slumber party. We were those girls silently enjoying their free show? Were they too embarrassed and too frightened to tell me? Did they try to stop me and I was really that drunk? These are questions that still blow my mind. But just in case that wasn't enough, the family's pet hamster died about two weeks after the party. Personally, I do not believe that the pee killed the hamster, but you try telling these corrupted traumatized middle school girls that.

Booty Bear Award

by Tracy W. – Brighton, MA, age 21

Well I have never been one to hide things from my friends, and now that I am in a sorority that is even truer then ever. See, if your not in a sorority, you would not know what goes on in the sorority house, meetings etc. You would probably just think of sorority girls as ditzy sluts, and the truth is what happens behind the scenes completely confirms that.

Every week at the meeting our sorority votes on the booty bear award. This goes to the most ridiculous hook up of the week it also allows everyone to catch up on the ridiculous events of the weekend. This award alone is half of my motivation to get buck wild, the other half is just that I enjoy it. The point though, is that the sluttier the story, the more inclined I am to share.

Anyway, I would say my sluttiest stories come from the two spring breaks I have been on in Acapulco Hawaii. During the first hour of my first trip there, I came to discover that anything is free if you let the Mexicans simply motor boat you. From cab rides, to pizza, to tequila, who would pass this up?

After a full night of Mexicans rubbing their sweaty faces in my cleavage, and loving every second of it, for whatever reason, I felt it was time to find a good looking American and make our way back to the hotel. The next thing I know I am in bed with the guy in the hotel room next to me the next morning. Not only the two of us though, we are somehow sandwiched between two sorority sisters. Now do not get me wrong I love waking up to situations like this, but I did have a concern this time.

I knew what a sloppy mess I was before leaving the club, the ride home is when I believe the tequila really hit me. This hook up must have been a sloppy disaster, and I was not about to have a bad rep with the boys conveniently close for my whole vacation. I needed to show this guy how much fun I can be. Why not wake him up with a blow job? Yes, still have sorority sisters to my left and right. It ended up being a successfully fun wakeup, but I do have a few rules. I do not have any problem giving head but I do not swallow unless I am very drunk.

So my next mission was to find something to clean up with. Thank God everyone was passed out. I went towards the bathroom to get a towel, but then I thought. What if someone needs that? I would not do that to my friends. But then my mind really kicked in. And it was still not passed 9 a.m. Sara was staying in the room with us. Now Sara is one of those girls that is the opposite of fun, good for holding on to room keys, and definitely travels to Mexico with granny panties. Kill two birds with one stone: clean up after my new friend and get rid of those terrible granny panties. And that is exactly what I did. Sara eventually found out, but it was not until the next sorority meeting when we got home.

Costa Rica

by Julie S. – El Paso, TX, age 22

When I was 18, I went to Costa Rica on winter break with my older cousins and stayed at their families beach house. The so-called party town was the next beach down from the house, which was basically a strip of bars and discos. The previous 4 nights I had hooked up with 2 Costa Ricans and 2 Americans. I just made out with those four guys, but that night, I ran in to an American named Greg, who I apparently really connected with.

Greg along with his nameless Americano friend, my cousin and I went to another disco down the street, where we continued to dance and mingle. One thing led to another and Greg and I decided to take a walk on the beach which was literally 10 steps away from the disco. So there we were schmoozing and boozing on the beach. Eventually starting to make out and shortly after starting to get physical. Greg peeled my top off first and then proceeded to take off his and lay it down for me. I plopped my ass down on his shirt, he lifted up my skirt and we started to go at it like Lohan and Ronson.

I swear, just as he was about to bust, I look up to find a light shining on our semi nude bodies. The light belonged to none other than a Costa Rican police. Greg immediately jumped off leaving me sprawled out with my skirt practically above my head. While I'm trying to pull down my skirt, there's the copper lets call him Officer Martinez shining his light right around my cha cha area. All the while, I am scrambling to get my shirt back onto my exposed body. Then Officer Martinez so eloquently asked what the fuck, we were doing having sex right in front of the club on the beach where people could see us. I said sorry and that we were leaving, to which Martinez responded with a long drawn out nooooo.

Opting for a different approach, I started to speak to him in my messy Spanish. I am pretty sure it is at this point that he called me mama, and asked why we could not have just gone a few steps over from the street. Then Officer Martinez does the unthinkable and asks us how much money we have on us. I did not have any cash that night since my cousin was buying all my drinks along with my fellow American boys. Glancing in Greg's direction, I see him open his wallet which contained maybe 2 bucks American.

After confessing to our lack of dollars, he tells us that he is going to have to take us to the station. As we start walking with him towards the street his partner joins us, giving me another person to beg to free us. I pleaded with them to have a heart and let us go in the spirit of Christmas and New Years.

Neither Officer Martinez nor Deputy Gonzalez seemed to be in the holiday spirit, both ignoring my pleas for freedom. Having misplaced my sobriety some 4 days earlier, I thought it was time to pull out the big guns. I leaned in to give Martinez a big hug, which he somehow manages to finagle into a kiss. Seeing this as an opportunity, I returned the kiss in full. As we pulled apart, I started to laugh and sing out a final plea. Apparently my kiss was so full of liquor that it intoxicated him and he agreed to let us go free. And as for Florida Greg, he crowned me the coolest chick ever.

In the Closet

by Bethany D. – Kansas City, MO, age 19

I am only 19 so I have not had much time to rack up many slutty hook-ups, but the one that comes to mind as the sluttiest would have to be the time I became incredibly intoxicated at a fraternity party. I end up talking to this guy who shall be called Jonathan on the porch of the fraternity house. Anyway, Jonathan lives in a different fraternity house next door to where we were, so we eventually went over to his room to take shots. By us, I mean Jonathan, my roommate Denise, Devin's roommate Evan, another guy named Kenny, and me.

So we do a few shots of vodka and I get pretty drunk. I had started drinking much earlier at a concert. So Devin and I start making out and my roommate yells at us that we are being sloppy with the tongue action, so we have going on so we take our make-out show on the road to a room downstairs. Turns out, the room we were going to use was locked so we found this lovely little hall that went nowhere and had a closet at the end.

Chelsea Goldstein – www.chelseagoldstein.com

We continue the little game of tonsil hockey in a chair that we found in that lovely closet until we heard someone coming. By this time, the clothing I had been wearing had made its way to the floor as had Jonathan, so we quickly scrambled to the safety of the closet and shut the door and continued what we were doing. We tried to keep our voices down because we knew that there were other voices in the hall.

Turns out, the voices we heard were Evan and another fraternity brother of theirs. They thought it would be funny to interrupt us and decided to take the remainder of the clothing that hadn't been shoved in the closet with us. Evan also thought it would be a good idea to shove a chair in front of the closet door so we could not get out later. Anyway, Evan and the other guy left eventually, with my shirt in hand, so Jonathan and I resumed trying to have some drunken good times. That does not work very well when you can not even think coherently much less get things where they need to go. Eventually, we decided to go back up to Jonathan's room. It was then that we discovered that my shirt was missing and that we had been trapped in the closet from a chair shoved up against the door. So I am sitting in a closet, without clothes, with a guy that I barely know waiting for one of his fraternity brothers to set us free. It was a good night.

Jimmy and Jack

by Krystal B. – Middlebury, CT, age 19

It happened over a year ago and I still have not heard the last of it. I was seeing this guy Chris but had a huge crush on two of his friends Jimmy and Jack. One night Jimmy's parents were out of town so he had a bunch of the guys over and Chris brought me along. Chris and I ended up getting in a little fight during the night and he left early, and I decided to stay over. My night after he left consisted vodka of going back and forth between Jimmy's bedroom and his sisters bedroom where Jack was and hooking up with both of them the entire night.

It was the best night of my life. Jimmy has the body of a god and even though Chris got mad, it was totally worth it, not a bad way to lose my vcard I must say.

The Dorms

by Ashley J. – Long Beach, CA, age 19

It was a typical Friday night for me and my girl-friends. We went out party hopping after getting pre-liquored up in our dorm rooms. It was the third party that we settled on, we had gotten some free drinks at the first two so we were pretty drunk already, but we grabbed a drink anyway. I saw this guy there. I did not know him personally but one of my friends did, and I thought he was cute. I went up to him and we started dancing. The dancing then turned into a full on make out session right in the middle of the dance floor. He asked me if I wanted to come back to his room with him, and of course I said, heck yea.

Well, I was way smashed at that point, however I could still walk and function normally. When we got back to his room he offered me some Jager. I think that stuff is disgusting but why would I turn down some free alcohol so I had a few more shots. A while into the foreplay I had to ruin the moment and take a much needed pee break. At that point I had so much vodka, bee, and Jager in my system my pee would probably be similar to grain alcohol.

I stumbled out of his room, down the hall to the toilets. I was in a new hall so I was not too aware of the layout and when I came out of the bathroom I was completely disoriented. Every freaking door looked the same. I could not remember which door I came out of. I just made a quick and educated guess of which room was his, and I figured I could ask anyone who answered it where my boys room was.

I went up to the door which I believed was his and before the door was opened I got into a sexy pose. When it opened, there stood an even cuter guy than the one I was hooking up with. Anyways we just started making out and yea. Anyhow it was a quickie. I left his room and started down the hall to escape any embarrassment from guy number one, and I happened to run into him in the hall. What happened to you? Did you get sick or something he asked. Nothing happened, I responded quickly to avoid further questions. And we went back to his room and I did it again.

After that one, I decided on going back to my room to avoid any other random hookups or situations, which luckily I did. Because otherwise it would have turned from a slutty hookup story to a story of how I got something itchy. Because 1 in 3 people have a STD on my campus. The next day I happened to bump into both of the guys and I played dumb. I claimed I remembered nothing from the night before and in fact I did not even remember meeting them.

Hook up Chronicles - Vol. 1

Just the Tip

by Leah H. – Kenmore, NY, age 22

My ex-boyfriend and I dated all through high school and college. He dumped me last fall, and to my surprise he managed to find a new girlfriend only two months later. She was my friend. So as nothing but revenge I invited his roommate and frat brother to come visit me. With every intention of screwing him and my ex.

However when the moment came and he asked if I had a condom, and I did, I said no, his response was "So do you want to play just the tip?" He was serious. It took all strength in me not to laugh in his face. So when he was giving it to me, he decided to scream "OH GOD I AM GONNA COME". I mean seriously scream. This time I had to run to the bathroom to laugh to myself, and think oh God I can not wait to tell all my friends this one. I did. And now I am telling you.

He was like attack of the cuddle monster all night long. All I could think of was how to shimmy out of his death grip without him noticing, or how I could ask him to go sleep on the couch. Instead I lay awake all night hoping he would cop out early he did not. He stayed till the next afternoon. Upon his leaving I called my sister and all my friends laughing hysterically about how embarrassed I was for him. Now he will not stop calling, and I feel like a dude for not answering. I have made peace with it.

Beer

by Amber J. – Bronx, NY, age 21

I like to drink, a lot, and so do most of my friends. Naturally we got pretty hammered one night before going to a bar and then proceeded to stumble our way to the bar. There was not much of a selection of men went we got there so my roommate and I sat down at a table and started talking and such. About two hours into the bar and a lot more to drink, our other friends have left and we are surrounded by guys.

My roommate met an attractive guy who was very much her type, while I was left with his friend who was not so much of mine. I let him buy me a drink because I felt bad he was not the smoothest of guys. About 15 minutes later he asked if I would go home with him. I said no. He asked again. I said no again. He asked once more adding in the fact that he did buy me a beer. This time I thought it over I mean he did buy me a beer and with the amount of alcohol I had, this was a great reason to go home with him. So I said yes only because he had a movie I really thought I wanted to see.

Chelsea Goldstein – www.chelseagoldstein.com

We walk to his house and he tells me he does not usually do this because he has a girlfriend. I get the grand tour of the shitty apartment and then we lay on the couch to watch the movie. I see the opening credits and he is practically attacking me with his hands and mouth. Somehow, I do not remember in my drunken stooper, we go to his bed and you know. I then get up saying I had to be up early and get dressed. As I am doing the walk of shame back to my house, I realize I never got his name.

Please Teacher

by Laura L. – Milwaukee, Wisconsin, age 24

I am a graduate student working on a master's degree. Part of my program is to teach college students while I myself am only a couple years older. In other words most of my students are 18 to 21 and I am 24.

I had this student over the summer last year who would hang out after class with a couple others and smoke. It was no big deal. Until the next semester I was at the bar with the other graduate students in my program and I was hitting the cranberry vodka pretty hard. I run into this guy well call him Peter and he is like HEY! I think you like taught my class last semester.

Peter was out for his 21st birthday celebration. I said well hey. Let me buy you a shot. So we did a few and then we were dancing. Later on we went outside so he could smoke and I sat on a curb and before I knew it I was knocked over into a bush and he was shoving his way into my mouth. My girl friend was a bit annoyed that I was slutting it up with a former student so I got his number in secret. We made arrangements to meet up. I ended up back at his place. Peters place is a real mess. One of his papers was in fact on that show Man vs Wild and the other paper was about ending the War on Drugs.

Needless to say within an hour of showing up at his place we were smoking pot and beginning our heavy petting session. I was really into it. He had a nice cock and everything. Not to mention I was kind of turned on by his eagerness to please teacher. We moved from the living room upstairs by the way I hate spiral staircases now and moved to the typical college guy makeshift bed on the floor. A mattress covered with dirty blankets. It was really hot especially since he wanted to go downtown first, got to love that.

I am thinking this whole time somewhere in the back of my head though that this may come back to bite me. That is about the same time his roommate came home. It is also about the time my clothes are all over the floor and the only thing I have on are a pair of red high heels. Needless to say we finished up and I fell asleep hoping this roommate wouldn't spot me on my way to my car the next morning. Morning came and I had a terrible hangover. It was a lot of fun but Peter ended up wanting to call me every night after that and start going places as a couple. No thanks. Young guys are fun for a night, but not forever.

The Buckle

by Alexis T. – Detriot, MI, age 22

When I attended SCSU in 2005 I worked part time at the Buckle a clothing store. My team leader Jennifer and I left work at five hit up some 99 Bananas, then once the store closed we were inebriated and decided to go meet up with the intern at the Buckle and other team leader M and J.

The bottle of 99 was destroyed and all of a sudden four-some wildness for quite some time. 9:45 am rolled around, Emily and I completely naked on the bed and the men on the floor passed the fuck out. We had to open the store at 10. We woke up and put men's button up fitted shirts over our slutty tops from the night before, and went to work. Then our two co-workers came in at 11 am.

Goldschlager

by Melissa M. – State College, PA, age 26

My current roommate and I are alcoholics. One night we chose Goldschlager as our drink of choice and we starting pre-gaming. We took ten plus shots each and took with us the remainder of our bottle in a Poland Spring to the bar and needless to say after a few shots bought by random guys we were blacked out.

After slutting up the bar, I wake up and realize I am in the middle of sick foursome. I am fucking some random guy and I turn my head and realize my best friend is fucking someone 5 centimeters from me. I reach out and grab her titty and we finish. If you know what I mean, still 3/4 in the bag we somehow end up switching partners and going for round two.

When we realize how much of a prostitute we were being we realize it is time to go yet to our surprise it is a snow blizzard and we are stranded. The two random guys take us back to the bar but no cabs in sight. We get a random ride to another bar where this dudes girlfriend works and she kicks us out and beats the crap out of us accusing us of fucking her boyfriend. We start hitch hiking in the snow storm and find an old man to bring us home. To this day I think we drove home in a white pick up and my roommate thinks we drove home in a black jeep. We do not even remember what this guy looks like.

Clitoris

by Gina K.. – San Jose, CA, age 36

Honestly, I went on one date in two years. Two weeks ago the guy went to my high school, but I did not know him. My girlfriend said I would like him because I do not like party animals and like guys that are not robots that have emotions, not wussies, and are not broke. I have never dated anyone with money, being that I was a musician for 17 years.

On this date me and this guy were making out and the next thing I knew he told me that he had been with two men and that he goes to sex parties and loves polyamorous love now all of this is while we are half nakcd in my bcd wrong place, wrong time. I felt so shocked and appalled that he was talking about this instead of giving me the orgasm that he said he learned about in some three week clitoris hands on class that he took. I said to him "um, do you realize you have not touched my clitoris all night?"

It was so disgusting when I told my parents they were just like "why you Gina, you get all the weird ones" and honestly, if he had not been so unemotional of a guy. It could have been interesting to hear more and have him get into showing me his moves that he learned in this class but there seemed to be a part of his brain that was missing he was all technical about life. What he did but there was no passion or element that he had any emotion in him whatsoever which is even weirder since he is a yoga teacher.

I heard he is a one minute man at these swingers' parties and does not even really seem to know how to please a woman so I do not understand why he would be in these environments when he is so un-sexual. I thought at least I would get to have tons of orgasms but hell no. Thank God I did not sleep with him. I told this to my group of friends a week ago at a party and they were all dying laughing and freaking out because they had no idea he was so strange.

Basketballing

by Mary G. – Los Angeles, CA, age 33

I was bartending and met a college baseball player, you know they are all assholes that was 6 years my junior. He was on spring break, so I decided to show him and his friends around town and took them to the bars in the area. I ended up taking him home. I should have known with his age that his sexual maturity equaled his shoe size.

We dry humped on the stairs all the way up to my room all the while giving me massive rug burn. I proceeded to give him a nice little blowjob and then he had the nerve to fart. I could not help but laugh and said next time, warn me. We proceeded to have bad rabbit humping high school sex all night long. I woke up the next morning and realized I did not know his name. I snuck out of bed and checked his ID. I mean, I should at least know his name when I called him a cab to get the hell out of my house.

Bi-Mexican

by Katie M. – Scottsdale, AZ, age 33

So I had not had sex in quite some time, so I was ripe for the picking. I met some guy I picked out in a mixed club. I ended up getting my taco pounded by him. One month later I am at this super gay club and this guy goes, "Hey, didn't we have sex on JT's couch a month ago?" I said, "No, that wasn't me". Of course, the one time I get my chalupa filled it is a gay guy. Just my luck.

Doggy Style

by Crystal R. – Toledo, OH, age 22

I was getting it on with my boyfriend on my parent's house while they were at work one day lets just say my sausage wallet was getting a big Ben Franklin inserted in it. Next thing I know my two year old golden retriever hops on the couch and try to get in on the action. My dog Rex starts humping my boyfriend who was humping me. I felt like I was getting gang banged. As I started screaming and trying to get them both off it ended in my dog getting off my couch and my boyfriend by greeting my mom at the door. Moral of the story never have sex at your parents house at least if they have a dog with both balls attached.

Peru

by Jennifer J. – Laayette, NY, age 19

This past weekend, my Peruvian friend Monica asked me to go out with her to the Apple Festival a tradition in the town I go to school in. Arriving at 8:30, I asked Monica for the thousandth time what time the festival was closing and she assured me it closed at 11 at night. So we got in line for apple fritters, and after 15 minutes the loudspeaker said the fest was closing at 9. So we just decided to wait for the apple fritters and watch fireworks. Of course we went on to watch the mediocre fire display without fritters because they ran out of them two people ahead of us. So needless to say Peru needed to watch her step for the rest of the night because I was deprived of any tasty apple anything.

After walking the mile back to her car in the bitter New England cold, Peru decided she needed to do something to cheer me up. So in her mind, going to a 21+ all Latino bar was the way to go, and remember I was only 19.

We got ready in her Machu Piccu-inspired room, and then had an hour and half digital cam facebook photo shoot. After looking our Hispanic best for our social networking addictions, we drove the half hour to the club, and while Peru drove, my Puerto-Rican half was brushing up Spanish pick-up lines. After figuring out Ven conmigo al bano chulo I thought this night may end up good.

After promising the bouncer a dance and maybe more, I was having my first Bud Light while Peru choked down a Corona. I swatted off a couple of senior citizens before chatting them up enough for them to buy, and me to finish, a beer. I had about 6 when Peru told me I had enough. I was going to choke this bitch myself. But when she told me we were just relocating, not stopping the party all together, I was satisfied.

I got somewhat sloppy drunk and ended up doing more than dancing with the bouncer. He asked me if I wanted to take shots but it was in the backroom. Since I was not think about what it really meant I said yes. Somehow the shot turn out to be me showing him a good time with my mouth. At least my excuse was that I was drunk.

Later we went to another party only to find out it was us two girls, and two Latinos; one Peruvian boy, and one Mexican boy. Before I knew it, we were all on a queen sized mattress on the floor in front of a flat screen watching American Psycho. Now if that is not a mood setter, I do not know what is. By the end of the night, I had my first taste of a Mexican burrito, and perhaps Peruvian sweet potato and I think I liked it.

Homeless Man

by Melanie C. – Louisville, KY, age 20

This happened just before Christmas this past year. Went to a pretty big kegger with one of my best friends, who convinced her ridiculously good looking older brother he needed to go. By the end of the night I was the slightly more sober one who got to drive home in the blizzard that had been going for a few hours.

After an extremely long drive home in which we could not see out of my windows and had them all down we arrived at my friend's house where she and her brother were staying. He lets her out, and hops back in the car, gives me an extremely drunk sloppy kiss and says, "So we going back to your house or what?" So I tell him what the hell, why not. Then his sister starts calling, she was wasted way more than the rest of us and asking him where he went? Is he going to fuck me? Doesn't he remember they have church at 9AM? And he tells her oh Lindsay's making my pasta. Yup pasta and hangs up on her.

We get back to my apartment and quickly undress and start making out like horny middle schoolers, he has me pinned to my wall ready to fuck the hell out of him, when he sets me down and goes, "Are we really going to fuck?" I nod at him like are you seriously asking me this? Which is when he starts hunting for a condom, since I am not in the habit of bring home boys randomly I don't have one.

And he decides to take my car to go get one from somewhere that is still open he spent a good 15 minutes trying to get it unstuck pushing it out of the ditch it is in, before giving up coming inside and wandering into my roommate's room and asking for one. My car was not stuck, the E brake was on and he was just too drunk to know it. Well my roommate did not have one, or was not conscious enough to understand the question, so we fucked anyway, three times. And then I got to drive him home.

So the next morning rolls around, and my roommate walks into my room when she wakes up and asks me if I had a guy over last night, and as it is a friend of ours brother, I say no why do you ask? And she is like some guy walked into my room in the middle of the night last night, reeking of beer and asked if I had a condom, and then she comes to the conclusion that absolutely kills me, "OMG Lindsay! There was a homeless man in my room last night asking for a condom we have to move!" I let her think that for almost a week, before his sister found out and told every one we knew how I banged her brother. Ironically she was not mad at all, she asked me how many times and if he was any good and when I told her she made this yeah noise only all manly and proud.

Lump

by Tara M. – Eugene, Oregon, age 25

I got a drunken booty call from my ex boyfriend. I being drunk myself gave into the revolting offer. After the deed was done and we passed out. In the morning as I start to wake up, wondering why the hell I am where I am I feel my ex making weird grunting noises. I thought nothing of is because I thought he was just waking up with morning wood and getting excited. We proceed to have morning wood sex. After the 30 seconds was over he got up off the bed.

When he stood up I looked over at the bed where he was laying. There was a lump of shit smeared into the bed. I looked at him and he proceeds to ask me if I farted. I said "um no you fucking shit the bed!" He was horrified, I was grossed out and in conclusion I never gave into his booty calls again

Catch Phrase

by Natasha W. – Corte Madera, CA, age 27

Two summers ago a bunch of my guy friends rented a house on the Cape and invited people up for the 4th of July. That night we all went out and it was kind of a disaster of a night but we all made it back to the house and decided to play Catch Phrase. I do not know if you have ever played it but drunken people make it even funnier. The point of the game is to describe the word that shows up on the screen and have your teammates guess the word before the buzzer goes off. If your team guesses it you pass it to the other team and so on until the buzzer goes off.

Long story short, I got the word that was the name of my "fuck buddy" if you will he of course was there and playing the game. Because I was drunk and the irony of the word I had to describe I just started laughing and pointing at my fuck buddy not thinking that people would yell obscenities as I pointed at him: "AIDS carrier" "Meathead" "Retard" "Whore" "Idiot" and the list goes on.

So my fuck buddy takes the game and throws it against the wall and proceeds to storm out of the house and of course I go running after him because I feel bad and because I was pissed this might have ruined my chances of getting laid that night. I told him we would take a walk to calm him down. We weren't close to the beach so we decided to take a walk around the neighborhood.

We ended up having sex in someone's yard and then a mini van drove by probably with a family in it so we ran, then we tried doing it up against a tree but this time the headlights caught us. We finally made it back to the house where we fucked on the picnic table as the sun came up. Needless to say, he was not mad anymore and I was completely satisfied. We also liked cars, beaches, showers, really anywhere we could go, but a public restroom because that would just be super gross.

Chelsea Goldstein – www.chelseagoldstein.com

Front Yard

by Veronica R. – Lee Summit, MO, age 23

The Homecoming: Who needs a bed, couch, or car when you have a front yard?

My senior year homecoming story is definitely one for the books. After the dancing had ended, the drinking continued. My boyfriend the same one I still have and I drunkenly made it back to my parent's house only to pass out on the couch watching SNL. At 4 a.m., and I wake up. My efforts to wake up Walter fall short, so I decided to take a different approach, a more hands on approach if you will. Well, of course one thing leads to another, and then I get a bright idea, "Hey, it would be kinky to do it on the front lawn." So we make our way to the front lawn, still dressed in our homecoming clothes, to get our kink on.

Now for my shining moment, my dad, who has internal alarm clock, is set at 5am, having no way of knowing, goes to check to see if the paper has arrived. As he peeks out the front window, low and behold, he sees me, his only daughter and her boyfriend boning in the lawn.

My dad still jokes about this which is better than any other alternative, he jokes at dinner in front of my mom, at Christmas, and any time he feels necessary. But I love him to death because he never told my mother, which I appreciate because I was spared a verbal lashing of being called a whore.

Best part that was our first canoodle of the relationship, and he did not find out that my dad knew until 6 months later. Hopefully, that made you laugh. It still makes us laugh years later.

In The Woods

by Kara D. – Manhattan, NY, age 20

My slutty ways date back to age 13. When I would give older guys head before school in the woods. I told my mom I was going to school early to sell candy before homeroom. She believed me and this went on for about two months. Keep in mind. I got boobs in 5th grade. All the guys wanted me, and by guys, I mean older guys. It gets better.

One morning I arrived at Paul's one of the five older guys I hooked up with house for our morning ritual. We would start walking to school, hide behind a tree somewhere, and I would drop to my knees cliché, I know. This morning was unlike any other. Paul answered the door in his boxer shorts, Come in, babe. I went in, being the slut I was, and we headed to his room. Are your parents home, I asked. He replied "They are still sleeping, they do not know anything."

As I walked into his bedroom, there were two people in the room making out naked. I knew the girl from school, she was older, and slutty of course. I had never seen the guy before. Later I would find out he was some hot mess high school drop out who smokes a lot of weed. We lay down in his bed he took his pants off and said go for it. I was so out of my comfort zone because I was used to doing this in the woods. The two random naked horny kids didn't help either. It kind of felt like a scene from a movie that my parent's wouldn't let me watch but I'd watch anyway.

I went ahead and did my thing. After I finished we sat on his bed with the lights out. His neon Nudes Live sign sure brightened up the room. The awkward naked couple, who had yet to speak to us, started smoking marijuana. The girl pulled a blunt right out of her back-pack. They took a hit, and passed it our way. Paul took a hit, and passed it to me. I do not smoke I anxiously replied. They all started laughing. Keep in mind I am 13 and these other pimps and hoes are about 15 to 16. I was so embarrassed, and they found it quite amusing. Fuck you guys I said. They just stopped laughing and the girl said something along the lines of, you are the biggest slut in 7th grade, everybody knows it. Well I could not really argue with her. We left for school and that never happened again. I still did give head in the woods before school for next couple months.

Years later, after my slutty days had past, I found out Paul went to jail for selling cocaine. The girl who pulled out the blunt works at McDonalds AND the local strip club. I think I am the only one from that neon lit room with a normal life.

Toes

by Carrie R. – Hayward, CA, age 27

I was hooking up with this beautiful, sensitive, 6'2" artist and teacher, a former yoga instructor who had the body of a Greek god. Sleeping with him too apparently I was not paying all that much attention to his anatomy. One evening we were watching a movie at his place. He was aware of my back pain due to my stressful career as a business owner so he decided to give me a shoulder massage, how considerate of the poor bloke.

He propped up on his sofa and I went on to sit on the floor between his legs. So he starts massaging my shoulders gently. I ask for him to go deeper into my tissues, I enjoy the pain. So he starts digging in deeper, I clench my hands around his feet since they were the closest things to grab. My eyes were shut the entire time and I was in a deep frame of mind, enjoying the feeling of every knot being released. As I slowly released my hold I started rubbing his feet simultaneously. We are both fully engaged in being in tune with one another, but suddenly my fingers felt a different sensation. I am running my fingers across his left foot I feel his toes I am rubbing my fingers across his right foot I feel a large clump. Instantly I feel our energies coming to a crashing halt. Being the curious pussy cat that I am, I decide to dig in deeper trying to figure out if he had his right foot's toes curled up causing the clumping effect.

Suddenly I start brainstorming my eyes are still shut and he is starting to become nervous I start backtracking if I had ever seen him with his socks off, and sure enough, nope. I start trying to get my fingers underneath his right foot trying to pull those toes out from underneath the curl. He starts spreading his legs wider away pulling his feet away from being directly beside me. Now I have grown completely suspicious. I arrive home and start going through his pictures on facebook. He had one image on a beach in Hawaii doing a yoga move, barefoot. He was so far I had to save the image to my desktop and zoom in. Sure enough, his right foot was shorter than his left. He had missing toes. Of course it is a sad situation and it must have been traumatizing having to go through such experience but lordly lord did I run off and call all my girlfriends and shout, he's got missing toes!

Naturally, he withdrew contact and started acting aloof trying to cover-up his insecurities. Being the emotional girl that I am I start attacking him via text for avoiding me and decide to point out, btw I noticed your lack of toes, wonder what the story behind that is.

"Ouch!" He tells me he had a bomb explode on his foot when he was eight years old in Lebanon. How sad!

I felt bad and decided to see him again, he grew even closer feeling comfortable having spilled the beans. My curiosity did not end there, I asked him to pull his sock off. He questioned if I was ready, I though to myself how bad can it be. So he pulled it off and bam. It was shaped like a giant vagina. There was a big hole where his toes should have been and the top of his foot resembled the vulva gathered on each end and sewn together. I did not know how to react. I truly did feel awful, but it is almost like wanting to laugh at a falling person, you just can't help yourself sometimes. So I tried to swallow it, and went on to caress his foot. Poor thing felt so comfortable.

We tried watching another movie after eating sushi at his place, mind you the food was still on the table although we had finished eating, this bloke decides to prop his feet on the table which was in my view of the TV. Now I am trying to avoid staring at his vagina shaped foot that is in the way but I just couldn't seem to stop. He caught on.

In the end it did not work out for other reasons but man oh man I have never experienced such a surprise like this. I do not mind sharing his name so you can investigate and track the missing toed guy, but I would hate to put him on the spot. I Think I have caused too much damage as it is. After all, he did mention he is a hyper-sensitive crab (cancer).

Carpet Munching

by Nichole M. – Columbia, MO, age 26

When I was in college I joined a sorority, really not my scene but I like to drink and knew I would be able to party nonstop. One day after I became a sister I came out to everyone becoming the target of anyone who wanted to dabble in a little carpet munching. Apparently most straight people that have gay friends would think, "Hey, you are gay and I have a friend who is gay, you guys will love each other." This is never the case.

One night at a mixer, my one sister brought her friend who just happened to be gay to set me up with. I took one look at her friend and I was grossed out. If I wanted to hook up with someone who looked like a man I might as well sleep with men it would save money on strap on. I like my lesbians of the lipstick variety.

When my sister asked me what I thought of her friend I said I was more attracted to her than her friend. Plus her friend's name happened to be my moms and grandmas, not fun for screaming out loud in the throws of passion.

My sister's friend took this as a come on and jumped my bones right there in the frat house. She wasn't bad looking and I was drunk and horny. We ended up having sex ein the game room while a bunch of guys watched. Not my proudest moment but it was pretty memorable.

Blocked Calls

by Candice R. – Charlotte, NC, age 18

I was at a Rehab concert at a bar in the city with my friend and her boyfriend. When I go to concerts or anywhere, my primary objective is to find a single guy who is at least 21 to buy me drinks all night. I am 18 and just graduated high school, but my story is always that I am a 20 year old ceramic art major at North Carolina State.

It was really easy this night because I was obviously a third wheel, so the guy came right up to me while I was standing by myself. Plaid Shirt Guy got me sufficiently drunk and we made out in the concert for a while, and then headed out to his car for the real thing. While I was redressing, he was giving me all these lines about how he was glad he met me, I am awesome, blah blah blah, but he had a confession to make. He had a 3 year old kid and I should meet the kid sometime. I love kids, but no thank you we are done now.

I still maintain that I did not give him my number that is not my style, but the next day I got a voicemail that said, Hi Melissa, this is Meagan. You do not know me, but you need to call me back as soon as possible. I called her back because I did not realize who she was, but she turned out to be Plaid Shirt Guys girlfriend, the pregnant mother of his child. She was pregnant with his second and due in just a couple weeks. She asked me about Plaid Shirt Guy and what happened between us. I fudged a few details to try and help him out a little, but she still left him. She left another voicemail a few days later telling me she hoped I was happy with myself, that I was the reason she had to leave Plaid Shirt Guy and move her kids to Tuscon to live with her parents.

A couple days later, Plaid Shirt Guy called me. By this point I knew not to answer if I didn't recognize the number because I did not want to talk to these people directly, so once again I got a voicemail. He said that because he is single now, we can start our life together and I should come over soon because we have such great chemistry. And that is the story of how I discovered you can block numbers on a cell phone.

Kettle One

by Kathleen G. – Narragansett, RI, age 20

It was sometime in February that a friend from college was throwing a birthday bash at some underground club for his twenty fourth birthday. My two girlfriends and I were iffy about going there because we all at one time or another in our school career hooked up with the birthday boy and did not want to be faced by him during a time of his celebration. Despite our efforts to try and not go, we ended up having to show our faces, for at least a half an hour.

So we get dressed in the hottest clothes that boost our best assets and call a cab to bring us to the party. The party started around eleven at night. We stroll in, casually late of course, at around one in the morning. Expecting the party to be at its peak of the night, it ends up we are the only three women of the fifteen guys in the whole place. The birthday boy comes over with a huge smile on his face to greet us and begs us to stay and have a few cocktails. We politely agree, knowing alcohol will make this party much more of a party, if you know what I mean. After paying top dollar for what looked like to be Barbie sized cocktails, we found ourselves at the liquor store next door buying a bottle of Ketel One vodka and smuggling that into the club to mix with the tiny drinks we were being served.

Only about twenty minutes later the three of us drank the last sip of the bottle and moved onto the dance floor. The birthday boy came to join, and danced his way in between me and one of my girlfriends. We were obviously blasted from just downing that bottle of vodka and became very touchy feely with the birthday boy.

He jumped at the opportunity of us being drunk and asked us to join him back at his house for an after party. One my girlfriends we shall call her the smart one, said no and immediately took a cab straight home. However, my other girlfriend and I stupidly agreed to go with him. So the three of us hopped into his two door eclipse, and headed back to his house.

We could not even make it out of the car when we got all erotic and started to grab the birthday boy and pulled him into the back seat. My girlfriend and I rubbed him every which way and even got his pants off. One thing led to another and we were all naked in the backseat. After some pretty heavy petting and some loud screams we heard multiple doors slam outside. So we quickly grab some clothes for cover up and look out of the fogged up car windows. All we see is about twenty of the birthday boy's friends standing outside wondering what was going on. How embarrassing. That was the last time my girlfriend and I have seen the birthday boy, and the last time we drove down his block.

Tanning Bed

by Stacey S. – Oxford, MI, age 31

I have been going to a tanning salon for close to two years and have formed a "friendship" with the guy that works there and he now owns it. He is totally hot and dumb as a rock and in December 2007 he approached me after my session to go in one of the tanning rooms to make out. It was pretty hot until I had to hide in the corner of the room when a customer walked in.

I have to say he has got a sick body which is not too hard to resist. We still hookup every time I go in, and it is always after I tan, which is kind of odd and I have been in some compromising positions. One time he left a souvenir on pants before I had to go to a work meeting.

My friends tell me they are never going to tan there ever because he and I have left our mark in most of the rooms. By the way I am also sleeping with someone else too. But I know the tanning guy is a sure thing and it is kind of exciting sneaking around.

Construction Zone

by Julia H. – Gurnee, IL, age 35

I am the district surveyor for construction zones in our local area. It is my job to go out and monitor the progress that is made, ensuring quality and safety for our citizens. You could say that I am an unlikely candidate for this job, but after years of 'persuasion' I was finally offered the job. I am unlikely because I am a woman. Not just any woman. I am a true hottie. I am 5'4 with long blonde hair and the deepest blue eyes, and a body that does not quit. Put me onto any job site and I could have those men building me my own bridge.

It was mid-July and I had been asked to check on a particular site that seemed to be taking longer than usual to finish. Being a nice night, I decided to take my 883 Harley out to inspect. Might as well enjoy a nice ride while I am working, right?

As I cruised down the highway I could tell that I was definitely in a mood for some hot and kinky fun. It had been awhile, I may look good but I am selective.

The vibrations coming from under me were really turning me on, so I made it a point to do my inspection and go out on a little prowl. Little did I know.

I arrive to the job site, and as I survey the destruction and torn up road, it is clear that they are on the path to rebuilding. There is fresh concrete surrounded with guardrails to prevent anyone from getting into it so that it will dry effectively. Now it is not unusual for cement companies to have an employee stay after hours to 'babysit' the cement, but when I saw the employee that they had selected my stomach felt funny. Just looking at her my stomach felt like I was riding in an elevator.

She was taking a much needed break when I noticed her. Sitting on the hood of the company work truck, her legs hoisted up on the bumper. She was a flagger for the cement company and she had the hottest red spiral curls in her hair. I had seen her before; she has been working for this company for awhile. Though I had never really had a chance to formally meet her, I had definitely always wanted to. I am admittedly bi-sexual and this was one woman that I would surely love to get a chance to explore. Tonight I had an excuse to talk to her after all I was there to inspect the progress.

We made small talk for awhile, me asking her questions about the job and walking around to look at what had been done. She was wearing Levis and a tank-top with a beautiful lace bra underneath. Her bra strap kept falling off of her shoulder and I could not resist reaching over to move it back up. Her skin was so soft and she smelled so good, I was already wet with anticipation. She looked at me with surprise but gave me the most seductive little smile I knew that it was all good. Reaching over to me she took my hand and led me back to a secluded area of the site.

Once we were away from the light I pulled her to me and kissed her. Her lips quivered and she was breathing heavy. Our tongues danced around each other, calling out to each other for more. I ran my fingers up and down her arms, letting my thumbs just barely graze across her breasts. Her breath would catch every time as her body arched into mine.

I began to massage her firm breasts through her top and then, having to have more, I pulled her top off. This girl had the most beautiful bronze skin, even in the shadows where we were, I could see it. I reached around to undo her bra, revealing two very enticing nipples.

Circling my fingers around them we kissed some more, both of us moaning with desire. She began to rub herself through her jeans which lit me on fire. I slowly moved my mouth down her neck toward her begging nipples. Moving fairly from one to the other I gently kissed, licked and sucked on each nipple until she was grinding her body against mine. She had started working her way up under my top, feeling her way toward my inviting nipples. I just had to have more of her first.

Pulling her down onto some moving blankets, I began to undo her jeans. Her panties were soaking wet, making my mouth water. I massaged her dripping pussy through her panties making her crazy with desire. I slid her jeans and panties off and ran a finger along her wet and slippery slit. It was so smooth that I kept doing it, pleasuring her breasts while putting my finger just barely inside of her. She was bucking against my hand, begging me to make her cum.

Getting comfortable between her beautiful spread legs, there was just enough light to see her glistening juices. I leaned my head in and began to lightly lick her lips. Slowly circling the special spot that she was aching for me to find to pleasure. I worked my tongue in gently and licked my way up to her throbbing clit, making small soft circles around it. I could tell that she was close and needed to cum, so I inserted just one finger into her while I continued my love-making on her clit. Licking her and fingering her slowly she worked up an orgasm so intense that her whole body was shaking. She was gasping for air, spreading her legs as far open as she could get them and holding my hair while rocking her hips against my face. Her juices were flowing all over my face, finger, and the blanket below us as she moaned with incredible pleasure. I lapped up as much as I could get, not wanting her pleasure to end. But she had different plans.

Sitting up slowly she pulled me to her, wanting to taste herself on my mouth. She kissed me deeply, inhaling her scent while reaching around to undo my bra. So softly she grazes her hands over my nipples. My nipples have always been an intensely sexual part of my body. A person could make me cum just by licking and sucking on them long enough. And the attention she was giving them had me dripping with anticipation. Rolling me onto my back she begins to kiss my tits, like a hot French kiss. One nipple and then the next. Slipping a finger in my completely wet pussy she starts to move down over my belly and hips. And showing no shame she immediately dives right in. This woman could eat me like I have never been eaten before. She had the perfect combination of long licks and quick swirls; making sure to pay attention to every part of my pussy, clit and everything in between. She was licking my clit and fingering me so good I was rocking against her hand, when she just barely stuck a finger in my ass. I can tell you that I might cum again just by writing this, I came harder than I have ever came in my life. My orgasm was cosmic. Like a million stars shooting out of my milky way. After she had gotten every last drop out of my hot pocket she looked up at me, it was beautiful. I relieved her of her night shift and took her back to my place on my bike where we spent the rest of the night taking each other to pleasures unknown before. God I love my job.

Ben

by Alison W. – Johnstown, PA, age 18

One of my older friends invited me to a party with her friends. She said there would be people my age so I decided to tag along. The party was great and it over-flowed with hot guys. It was like a convention for Abercrombie and Fitch models. I felt really confident because I was wearing one of my favorite outfits which made me look like I wanted some but was not a slut or anything and I acted like I pretty much owned the joint.

I was dancing with a couple guys, until one guy and I really hit it off. We went into a corner and started to hook-up. His name was Ben and I guessed he was a bit older than I was but I did not know for sure and frankly I did not care. He was the best kisser and I was lucky that he was the one to stick his tongue down my throat. He was also the only guy I let feel the girls right off the bat.

We got a bit down and dirty with over the clothes action even though everyone could see, but we did not really care. Everyone was too drunk to notice dry humping in the corners of people's houses. I think he went under my shirt but I am not sure due to the beers that were consumed earlier that lovely evening. But let's just say he did. We hooked up some more and then talked for a while. He was really hot, funny, and nice and he didn't smell, so I felt like I hit the jack-pot.

The night was going perfect, and we were dancing like wild banshees to 90s techno who cared how bad the music is when you're drunk? By the end of the night we exchanged numbers after one last hook up of the night. I was going to wait till the next time we went out or saw each other to go further, even though it was pretty hard to tame the beast from such a hot piece of ass.

About two days later, after school I went to visit my dad at his office. I walked in and we were talking about how are days were when in walks Ben. We kind of just looked at each other in aw until he said, Oh, I did not know you knew where I was working! Great to see you again!

Apparently he was an intern working for my dad and he failed to mention that to me. I just looked down and said it is nice to see you too. It was not until my dad introduced me to him as his daughter that he freaked out. Luckily my father is not one to notice sexual and awkward tension between a teenager and her older boy toy from a couple nights before. Turns out he was much older than me which made our seeing each other something that was not going to happen. It was fun while it lasted!

My Wings

by *Christina G.* – Munich, Germany, age 18

My funniest and worst hook-up experience happened in high school. I had just begun in high school. I live in a city where there are three high schools, inclusive mine that invites each other to their dances. My friends and I drank a lot of alcohol before these parties. Of course everyone gets pissed ass drunk.

I had had a crush on a friend of a friend for a while, but had never done anything about it until that unforgettable night of horror. It was Friday and it was my high schools turn to host a party. My friends and I were warming up before the big night with allot of vodka shots, drinks, vine etc. I have been told that the guy I had a crush on was going to the party and I therefore decided that tonight would be the night.

Unfortunately I have never been lucky in games and this night was no exception, as my friends kicked my ass in various drinking games. Before we were about to go, my friends thought it would be funny to dress me in a Spice Girls t-shirt, an army cap and angel wings, and I, with my blood replaced with vodka, thought it was a fantastic idea.

When we got to the party, I immediately spotted my prince-charming and went over to say hi. Next thing I know the guy and I are on a parking lot near my high school doing the hanky panky. I could not really remember what had happened until then, but remember thinking, "What the hell, at least I did not miss the fun part." I have never been more wrong! Suddenly a patrol car drives up and two officers step out and ask us to get in the car which we did.

They took us to the station where we were told that some old lady had called them, because she thought he was abusing some kid. I could not really understand why she would think that, until I looked down and realized that I still was wearing my wings and spice girls t-shirt. My cap was lost in the heat of battle. At the same occasion I noticed that my arms and knees had big bloody wounds which I have gotten from the parking lot which apparently were made of gravel. I swear I have never felt as stupid as that very moment. But the guy I were with seemed pretty calm, so I did not wanted to make a fool of myself by making a scene.

After we had answered some questions, the police, as we both were living at home at that time, called our parents to come and get us. I promised myself that this incident would be filed under denial, since it had worked so many times before, and the next day when I woke up nothing would have happened. Then our parents stepped in, at the same time of course, and I sadly had to acknowledge that his father was my new high school English teacher. Great, three years with him!

It was the longest drive home ever. My mom did not say a thing, but I felt the burning letters in my forehead saying - WHORE! The next morning it was really difficult to be in denial as the leaves in my crack and the wounds were constant reminders.

My teacher never commented the episode, but it took me a couple of month before I could look him in his eyes again. I have met the guy a couple of time after, but it seems like he has lost some of his magic.

Til Dawn

by Emily W. – Redbank, NJ, age 29

Picture this: Fire Island, New York off coast of Long Island. August 2008. Ocean Beach. Following a soaking rain. It is early in the evening the island was ripe for fresh air and fun. While we may have missed happy hour in the bars our summer share shacks were bumping. Fast forward to nightfall and the start of marathon house parties.

Being the social, gregarious aka loudest person I am. I have no trouble meeting new people. My girls and I venture to a house we have never been to before. Over the next hour we schmooze, some canoodling but overall very tame. With little patience I am ready to move on. My girls stall. I am floating about and come across some cute guys.

Now, these are not frat boys, these are not drunkards, these are bonafide men and man candy at that. I peak, ignore and move on. Fast forward to the bar and the guys appear once again. We do the look see look away tango for a bit until finally someone remembers his cajones and approaches me. He introduces himself in such a cocky way.

We chat for a bit but I grow antsy and excuse myself to the restroom. I go to do a lap at the bar and see who has arrived since last I scoped. Fast forward to later and ran into each other ending in smooches. We are now at bar number three of the night. He takes my arm we go chat by the water. Than to the local bakery for some munches. He buys me a black and white pastry. We walk slowly in the direction of the share shack. More smooching, heavy petting, we are in the MIDDLE of the walkway, hands all over, people walking all over hmmm, what to do.

Genius notices an overgrown lawn not too far so we duck into the neighbor's jungle of a front walkway. A serious make out session and groping hands. He is really sweet actually, kind of pleading to play and I am all good girl and thinking it is 4 am and we are almost thru. All of a sudden he is down on his knees. He is ridiculously generous seemingly unselfish. Several times we freeze as we hear giggles a housemate is returning home and we are like barely wearing clothes. Thankfully they pass. More thankfully he is continuing to go down on me.

Eventually I realize the man must speak again and rescue his oral mechanism from certain medical intervention, to my chagrin, He is fantastically, ridiculously good. Being the happy camper he has made me, I want to return the favor but mind you we are rather exposed. Excitement gets the better of me. I tell him to brace himself and down I go. He literally braced himself on the neighbor's fence and garden chair. Considering the hours that have passed since he discovered no panties and the dancing vertical sex I was not at it for too terribly long.

At this point its getting chilly, it is also about sunrise. He mentions daybreak I go get my beach blanket and we meander to the shore. In long island there is only one lifeguard beach chair that remains standing all season. All the others are put down at the end of each day. We make our way to the beach near this single standing lifeguard chair. Needless to say the canoodling continues till the break of dawn. Sunrise was not the only thing coming that day.

Cowboy

by April C. – Charlotte, NC, age 35

It all started my freshman year I decided that with a new life in a totally new town that only really had beer and cows it was time for a serious relationship. I knew I did not have many options as far as the caliber of boyfriend I would be choosing. I had to pick between the player, the cowboy, the bartender, and the professor. I chose the cowboy. I have always thought that they were loyal, trustworthy, and since we were attending college-smart. Plus cowboys LOVE to party, that was my kind of guy or I thought so.

So I picked him and we fell in love for about eight months. We had a good steady relationship with lots of good sex too. He liked to go down a lot and I was happy with that, until our relationship got rocky. I was trying to straighten up my act so I did not flunk out of school and have to move back home, so I stopped partying as much and the cowboy did not. In fact he decided to start messing around with a couple of my friends and thought that I would not find out.

Unfortunately for the cowboy I did find out. I tried to figure out a way to dump him, humiliate him, or just hurt his feelings so bad that he would never cheat again. It took a few days and a friend from high school to do the trick. I racked my brain for a long time and asked others what they thought I should do. My mom told me I should just break up with him and let it go but that was too easy. The cowboy had broken my heart.

So one day, my friend from high school called out of the blue and said he would be staying in town with a mutual friend and thought if I did not have anything to do I should meet at a bar and have drinks with them. I was all for it, since the cowboy had made my life miserable. My friend was in the military and was just on leave at the time and had many stories to share about how much he hated the army and how he wished he had not joined.

I was telling him how sad I was and we just kept feeding off of each others sorrows while doing shots of tequila. We decided to take the party back to my dorm room where in my drunken stupor the idea came to me.

I knew what my revenge would be I decided to have wild sex with army guy I figured there was no harm, he was cute. I always wanted to do him in high school but never did. After we were done I did not make him wear a condom, gross I know, and army guy left, I called up the cowboy. He had to come right away because I really needed to "talk" to him.

When the cowboy arrived, I jumped on him and we started to do it which is when his love of going down made my revenge so easy. I know how disgusting I am, but I could not help myself. I got my revenge, broke up with him the next day, and he still does not know why.

Foam

by Megan W. – Sydney, Australia, age 25

I met one of my boyfriends in a nightclub at one of those bubble foam parties. I had my eye on him for a while. That night after encouragement from my good friends Tequila and Jack Daniels, I jumped his ass. We barely gotten past names when I pulled out his dick and started to play with it under the foam. Anyway things quickly progressed, but I wanted to make it a little more personal so we went to the restroom. After a good steamy fifteen minutes frequently interrupted by drunks busting to do a shadoobi, we finished up and headed home.

The next day though, due to the long time spent in the soap residue, which was obviously cheap, our skin dried out and started to flake, particularly in the genital region. The moral of the story is if you are going to get slutty, stay away from PH altering products.

Saleen

by Brandy R. – Linden, NJ, age 21

My friends and I call anyone we think is a lesbian and a big dyke, JUDY. If we are in public or whatever and someone looking suspicious we holler JUDDDY! We found on urban dictionary that it actually says that like 1 in 4 lesbians in the world are named Judy. We get a kick out of it, I actually met a lesbian Judy the other day it was fucking hilarious.

I was kind of dating this girl but not quit yet. We were fucked around then decided to attend this little gay party together. I went to the bathroom and this other lesbian that has a girlfriend name JUDY was in the other room. My current girl followed the other girl in and started making out with me. Before I knew it we slipped away in JUDYS badass Ford Mustang Saleen, and proceeded to pull the car off to a random lot and fuck me in the passenger seat of her JUDYS car. The new girl and I went back to the party like 20 minutes later. I was getting the worst looks from everyone it was a scandal, and I was fucking wasted.

Playing Through

by Heidi M. – Auburn, AL, age 20

So a few years ago, my boyfriend at the time and I liked to be spontaneous in bed, and we tried to have sex somewhere new whenever we did. It added some spice to the relationship.

One day, we decided to have sex on the golf course in my town. We walked over there and went onto the green having no clue where exactly on the course we were. Then we started making out and undressing. Keep in mind it is broad daylight, and a Sunday. We were really into it at this point, and in the middle of having sex, when all of the sudden we heard a noise. I thought it was just an animal in the surrounding woods or something like that, so we just kept going.

A few seconds later we both heard "ahhem!" and as we looked up, there were two men standing over us holding golf bags. We were in complete shock because here we were bare naked in the middle of a golf course with two old men trying to play standing right over us watching.

We immediately got up, grabbed our clothes, and without saying a word we ran for our lives back to his house. When we got back, we caught our breath, looked at each other, and burst out laughing for hours. We had sex in his bed that night.

Santa Monica

by Amanda W. – Hermosa, CA, age 36

This is not particularly slutty but I met the sexiest guy on the beach in Santa Monica. Two weekends ago he caught my eye due to his ridiculous hotness. The following weekend I saw him again on the beach while I was jogging and smiled and waved, he responded. The next day I saw him yet again as I was going to relax by the water and made a point to go and talk to him.

His name was as crazy as his pecs-Cornelius. I was not picking up any signals so I told him to enjoy his day. An hour later I looked up to see him smiling down at me on my beach towel. He and I live two blocks apart as fate would have it so he invited me to stop by on my way back home. Out of character for me but I did anyway. I figured the universe was throwing me a bone to make up for my last two experiences. We talked, shared some wine and I left. Later I sent him a text telling him it was a pleasure to meet him. He responded with "let me know if you want to come over for more pleasure." Let me just state for the record the man is hotter then David Beckham and has a body not meant for clothes. I sure as shit wanted more pleasure.

I went over there a little later we got naked and made out. His body is a magnificent gift. Christmas morning was never that good. He was perfect to look at but not at all what I was hoping for. I actually had to ask him if he wanted me to leave. I felt like he was not into it. He assured me was, he was hard and everything but he just was not as handsy or aggressive as I like.

I think it may have been a relatively new thing for him to pick someone up and move that fast, me too, but still, he kept asking me what I was thinking. I was seconds away from saying, actually I am here to sweat and scream not share my feelings. Again, out of character for me to be naked on some guy's bed hours after meeting but I was going with the flow. We stopped, his phone rang-and he answered it. I left shortly there after with plans for the following day. Needless to say he cancelled and then I got the I am too busy to give my time to anyone, it would be great to see each other but the timing is bad right now text.

All Over Me

by Jamie S. – Memphis, TN, age 22

I was hooking up with this one guy that I met at a bar and he came back with me to my apartment because he did not drive there. He was a bit ugly but he was the only guy at the bar who seemed to be desperate enough to buy me lot of drinks. Since I was intoxicated I had the beer goggles and liquor makes me horny. I was pretty pissed off at my current boyfriend. We went to get it on after the bar closed.

We are having sex and he tells me he is not able to get off so he pulls out and when I am sitting up I grab my boobs for a second and he tells me do not stop touching them. So I am thinking ok. So I keep massaging and rubbing my breasts then all of a sudden he starts to jack off and I was freaking out. So once I opened up my eyes and realized what he was doing. He splurged all over me!

Panties

by Stephanie D. – Woodlands, TX, age 19

This guy I know was cheating on his girlfriend for about four months until she found out. The story goes. We did not really like his girlfriend. We kind off made him cheat by provoking him I guess and so he would mess around with other girls.

One time he was doing this girl and he looks at the time and realizes that his girls going to be home any minute cause she would come to his place after work. He freaked out and makes her get out. She could not find her panties so he just kind of says "just go" an hour later the girlfriend gets home and sees the panties lying on the bed and she's like are those for me. "Aaaaw when did you go out and buy them?" and he is like "ooh I was just about to wrap them for you!"

She had no idea at that point so she is like putting them on a few days later and sees like a stain on it. It looks like piss or shit, I do not know because I did not really care to know. She spazzes and asks her boyfriend for the receipt which he obviously did not have she went to Victoria's Secret and started bitching out the girl at the register about them selling her used panties.

The lady at Victoria's Secret goes too her, "we have not sold these here since last Christmas" the girl just stares at the lady for a minute then turns bright purple and walks away, broke up with him the next day! Right now, I am pretty good friends with the girl now and we laugh about it sometimes.

Fat Lips

by Sandra A. – Beachwood, OH, age 19

I had a friend with benefits for two years. He cheated on all his girlfriends and sadly I cheated on all my boyfriends. He was a reliable lay and he knew how to use his big toy really well. You can't just give up amazing sex.

A while back I was with my friends with benefits at a house party. We went to a private place and I was a really drunk. This is pretty embarrassing I was giving the guy a blow job. I do not know how this happened but somehow his knee hit my lip and it started bleeding so I ran out of the room to go wash it off half naked. He ran after me in his boxers. People at the party got a nice laugh out of that one. They were probably thinking WHORE!

80 Bucks

by Stacy K. – St. Louis, MO, age 40

This story all starts out with me and my 17 year old, precocious to say the least, girlfriend's senior year. We decided on the hip Ft. Lauderdale for spring break. Well of course we had to bring all the right stuff with us like fake IDs with our huge pictures and Midwestern backgrounds. Who would ever figure us out?

We get there and find out our hotel has actual puke on the ceiling. Anything called the Bahama Mama Hotel should be expected to have that at least. After the second day, we were relived our parents bailed us out to stay at the Sheraton. We were trying to budget.

Our daily retreats were beach, drinking and drinking. Of course our fake IDs turned out to only work at the "She Bar" which we later found out was for trannys and gays. We realized this after a couple nights there and no one was hitting on us.

Well about the third night there we were eloquently walking the strip where, of course, all our late night pick ups were. I suddenly ran into this guy sort of Danny Tario was the lead male dancer for the show Dance Fever. He had a great head of hair and really tight pants on. Anyways he and his friends came up to our room to party. We were very cautious being the previous group stole clothes and money from us. The hottie asked if I wanted to come with them to their parent's condo in Miami which was about 45 minutes away. I hesitated and then said "why not" against my better judgment. My drunk friends said "go have fun" So glad my friends watch my back.

So we get to a cheesy motel and one guy says his parents do not want any guests over. So he dropped his brother off with me at this motel or whatever it was we definitely fooled around all night hardcore for the 80s and since I was a virgin, I think he gave up on me because when I woke up in the morning, I was alone. Oh shit I thought! How do I get back? Oh yeah, A taxi brainiac!

So I call my friends to tell them that I am stranded and they are mad I woke them up of course. They tell me just use the rest of your money. So I call a taxi and look in my purse. Oh Crap!!!! He stole my $80 a lot for the 80s. So I tried to keep it together and just went along with the ride. This guy stopped at shit you not, three places along the way. He got cigs at one stop. Stopped at some restaurant and then some house! I was terrified. We get to the hotel and I said, "Be right back, my friends have the money right inside the doors," and took off to my room as fast as a freaking Looney Toon! The guy came screaming after me. Somehow I lost him and got to my room and locked the door.

Would you believe I got a call a month later from the guy. He must have gotten my number in a drunken stupor that night and I was like, "why the hell did you leave me?" oh I was hungry! Click.

Hooker Boots

by Jasmine W. – Pittsburgh, PA, age 20

This past winter I was out with my girlfriends and of course was completely wasted. It took me forever to get ready and I had put on a slutty top, my shortest pair of booty shorts, and my tallest hooker boots. At one of the bars that my girls and I stopped at I happened to see my ex-boyfriend Paul.

Paul and I had been on and off for awhile and we were definitely in one of our off periods. I knew I looked hot and decided to flirt with him the entire night. Of course he took the bait. Paul kept buying me drinks the remainder of the night and I was taking shots like it was my job. At the end of the night we were both completely trashed. Unfortunately, the rest of my friends were fairly trashed as well so we could not find anyone to drive us to either of our apartments, which are both about twenty minutes away from downtown and the bar we were at.

One of Paul's friends volunteered to give us a ride to a nice hotel down the street. The roads and sidewalks were pretty icy. As we were getting out of the car, Paul slips, flies through the air, and falls right on his ass making himself look like a complete fool. The people at the front desk of the hotel did not even try to hide their laughter in. When we get inside Paul decides it's a good idea to pay the hotel with cash.

Remember, I am in my shortest pair of booty shorts and my hooker boots. Every person at the front desk was staring at me like I was a prostitute and Paul was a baller. When we got up to the room I stripped my clothes off and went to work on the boots. I could not seem to get them off so I just left them on and proceeded to hook up with Paul while I still had the boots on. It was probably the worst drunk hookup I had ever had. The next morning, my hair a mess and my make-up smudged, my walk of shame consisted of strutting past an entire room of hotel guests eating their continental breakfast.

I can guarantee that every single person choked on their food. At the front desk there was a whole new set of employees so I got three new people thinking I was a prostitute. I held my head high and got on the subway to go home. It being a Saturday morning, the subway was packed and I had to stand most of the way home. At the second to last stop I started to walk towards a seat that had emptied and my heel caught on the edge of a seat. Down I went into the lap of a guy that looked about my age. I think that was the only time a man was not happy to have me in his lap.

Beads

by Kristina B. – Flushing, NY, age 23

Sophomore year of college it was very easy to sneak in booze. I no longer to pretend to go the library with my loser looking computer bag to end up stuffing it full of Old English 40s. I could have guys in my room at all hours, no more security guards watching my ever move. I now was the in crowd invited to off campus parties. I was the SHIT!

Everyone knew me not by my first name but my nickname Pap. Not knowing that my name would be changed and not for the better. So when it was time for Mardi Gras I was ready to show my ladies and score some beads. And to add frosting to the cake my nipples were both pierced so I was pretty much on top of my game or so I thought.

The party was happening, kegs were pouring beer, sported a few nice sets of beads. That is when he came like a bat out of hell. The dickhead who ripped my beads off my neck. More than anything I stood there like a deer in head lights. Then this white girl went nuts, yelling, and worse spilling my Busch Light on the basement floor. I went after that needle dick but the crowds of people did not make matters better. Turns out bead boy is friends with my friend Jason. Any who bead boys name is Jeff.

As the night continues the Busch is really kicking in. I am dancing thinking I am such black chick. And then it hits me. I start to feel watery mouth. I take small then bigger swallows to fight back the urge to puke on the dance. Luckily my techniques of dealing with watery mouth are intact. I decide this hot mess needs some air. The back yard of the house kind of like a city dump. There is a refrigerator parked in the middle of the back yard. And would not you know bead boy Jeff pigeon style on top. I had found him, the fucker who stole my beads. But now he's looking pretty damn fine! I sit next to Jeff and light up a ciga-rette. We get to talking about how he stole my neck-lace. Then, out of nowhere we both get watery mouth and vomit. It was a cute little turn your head away, it was a full blown chunks. After pulling ourselves together, we start to make out. Nothing is better than fresh vomit to turn you on.

I'm out of breath not from making out with hottie Jeff, but from walking my fat ass up the hill to my dorm room with him. Talk about a complete turn around. In my room Jeff and I soon get hot and heavy.

I have always had this sick infatuation of using fun dip on a guy's dick. So Jeff was my practice dummy. The fun dip was some orange coloring and it was everywhere. On him, my shirt, my bra, fun dip every where. The next morning I woke up and there was Mr. Fun Dip sleeping on my futon of fun dip love. At least I didn't have the walk of shame with food coloring all over. Of course Jeff went back and told his friends. So Pap is out and Fun Dip is in. Every time I see dream boat Jeff or my other college friends all I hear is hey can I get some fun dip.

House Arrest

by Hannah B. – Ithaca, NY, age 34

Last weekend in the Hamptons this cute guy and I just met and wanted to hook up at this share house. There were no empty rooms with privacy, so we did it in a walk in closet while someone was showering in the bathroom, I made him bring in a mattress and a pillow. A few minutes later someone knocked and I hid in the back of the closet. After that we finally went to another room and started doing stuff, we thought the door was locked. The next thing you know my roommate came in, so we had to finish on the bathroom counter.

After that I was horny as shit and was so bored. I drove to a guy I met on Jdate dating website for Jews, who was under house arrest. We hooked up but he was really bad in bed. To this day he's known as house arrest guy.

A Sticky Situation

by Erica A. – Rochester, NY, age 34

I tell my girlfriends everything. One time at the end of a singles weekend I was still horny and I was not satisfied. This guy and I wanted to hook up but we already checked out of our rooms. We went to the women's bathroom and I started giving him a hand job there, then all of the sudden I hear banging on the door. It was a female security guard says, "WE HAVE A SITUATION HERE" into her radio. He was escorted out of the hotel I did not mind so much because he was not so big and a little hairy down there and my hand was getting so tired.

Chelsea Goldstein – www.chelseagoldstein.com

Outback

by Kayla R. – Atlanta, GA, age 18

I had the balls to work at the disgusting restaurant named Outback. A huge mistake. I was only 16 and still a virgin. I was a little horny you could say. Everyone that worked at outback was older and fucking retarded, but I guess that just turned me on for some reason.

I was a hostess and I would always go to the kitchen and lift up my long black skirt just to show the 24 year olds what illegal piece of ass they were missing. This went on for a while until I was asked to come to their apartment and apparently to have a good time. I thought what the hell, free alcohol. I go and find my coworker Ryan and this other worker Sean. Sean was the first to confront me and to start offering me drinks. Just to get in my pants, which really was not a problem except that he had longer hair than I did. He kept grazing my vagina and I was getting real fucking sick and tired of his long dirty nails scratching me every time he did, so

202

I moved along to my other friend Ryan. Ryan was an average guy, except he was from somewhere in Canada and had a sexy accent.

The second I started talking to Ryan he asked me to give him a lap dance, and I was just like. Honestly what the fuck is wrong with you. I mean I guess I usually would but I did not want the other coworkers there to see a 16 year old giving a 24 year old a lap dance. I was just weirded out so I got drunk and then left just to be even hornier when I got to work the next day. I wore my short skirt to work that day and decided to go on break early. Ryan was in the back changing into his work clothes so I thought what a perfect opportunity to get some.

I grabbed Ryan and pushed him into the cooler in the kitchen and we started hooking up. I started taking his pants off and as soon as I took his boxers off. Literally I couldn't stop fucking laughing at his two inch dick. I was so amused and disgusted I immediately put my shirt on and got the fuck out. Just in time to find the long haired freak Sean in the changing room. I thought what a nice change hopefully this one has a bigger dick than a baby. I pretended I had to change and started to rape Sean. Although Sean really wasn't any better considering he asked me if I wanted to have sex outside behind Outback. Rather then on the dirty floors of the changing room. That fucking did it. I mean why the hell these old men were so fucking stupid. I could not handle any of it anymore and did not want to be embarrassed anymore. I just walked out of the restaurant and never came back.

Dakota

Meagan M. – Oklahoma City, OK, age 23

I have been going out with my boyfriend Chris for two years. He is sweet and what you call a "Geek". We are not talking about the pocket protector and suspender wearing guy though. When we first started going out I was his first everything. First kiss, first make out, and first time. The truth, we were each others first times actually.

Well I have a dog Dakota. Every time Chris kisses me he gets extremely jealous. I do not know if you have pets or this has happened to you. But one night we were getting it on my aunt was not home and then I heard my door bedroom pop open thinking oh shit someone came home. Nope it was Dakota my dog, and he jumped on the bed and got between us. And tried humping me and my boyfriend, we were like, What the FUCK! DAKOTA! DOWN!!! Then he started bringing an arsenal of his toys in wanting us to play. We eventually stopped having sex. Thanks to the damn dog.

Chelsea Goldstein – www.chelseagoldstein.com

The Stall

by Erin Y. – Rapid City, SD, age 32

I was 19, and it was my birthday, so a few friends and I go to this new bar with our fake IDs. We get there and wow what a party after our 6th pitcher of beer I go downstairs to play pool where I meet this guy, after a while he introduces me to his girlfriend she is very hot too.

After a few more drinks this guy and I sneak off to the store room. This guy can use his tongue and I know this is not slutty enough. The night goes on his girlfriend and I meet up in the washroom, we take over the handicap stall because you know there's tons of room in there. We take turns going down on each other she screams that she's coming and her man comes in the room, thank God it was a big stall. I never knew what I could do standing up.

The night is done and my two new friends and I are totally happy with the evening. I join my friend and her man again and continue our party. My birthday party, we all hop in a cab and this couple I picked up wants to come along, I ask my roomies if they could come. What all 5 of us did in our living room unbelievable till this day still can't believe what happened. That was the best birthday I ever had. In the end I had 2 guys and 2 girls to make my 19th year special all in one night.

Wii

by Rachel M. – Winter Park, FL, age 21

I had recently turned 21 and so some people I went to school with decided to hit the bars. I get completely shit faced and ended up meeting this ugly dude. And of course I had my beer goggles on. I end up going home with him. All I remember is Playing WII Mario Cart, and scarfing down some late night calzones.

I wake up next morning naked next to the dude with a used condom next to me. He wanted more sex and I gave in. Hating myself. Then I ask him to take me to my car. We go back to the bar we were at, and search and search for my damn car. I had no idea where I parked it. So I am driving up and down, everywhere trying to find my car so I don't have to look at his face anymore. Finally find it an hour later, in the complete opposite place we were looking in. I literally lost my car. I felt like Ashton Kutcher in "Dude, where's my car?"

Carriage Ride

by Heather T. – San Francisco, CA, age 35

I was planning on going to a psychic gathering with my best friend Marianne when we decided to stop off and say hello to her husband and his business associate at this little Tapas place; not topless, Tapas!

We walk in and I sit down next to this guy that looks like he was ordered straight out of a Latin soap opera. He was very yummy from head to toe with an Argentinean accent. I mean even Lorenzo Lamas on his best day in the 80's couldn't hold a candle to this guy. I was instantly smitten and giving my best pout and sexy smile. My friend was even flirting with him in front of her husband. I gave her the "Back off bitch this one is mine" stare. Sebastian was a vineyard owner from Argentina and was in town to talk to my friend's husband about distributing wine. Whatever, I was all about having him distribute something else.

We start drinking all these different wines and eating cheese and somehow seemed to forget that we were stopping by on our way to get our fortunes read and talk to dead people. Five or six bottles of wine later and nearly midnight it is pretty obvious where this is headed. But then it gets interesting. We stumble outside to go to our next destination, when the horse and carriage pull up. I shit you not, it was like right out of Cinderella, well almost, and except the husky woman driving that team of white horses was the local lesbian that was in love with me.

She offers to give us a carriage ride and we climb on board so I have this hot Latin American guy sitting next to me and my friends across from me and the love struck lesbian driving us around. We go by my friend's house and get seven more bottles of wine and before you know it I am making out with the Latin guy in front of everyone and anyone that is driving by.

We were like super glued together and it was hot. Unfortunately the lesbian got so upset that she chugged two bottles of wine and became so drunk that we had to then in our intoxicated state get her 250 lb ass into her truck, unhitch her horses, load her horses and carriage into the trailer, and then drive her hillbilly ass back to the country. Listening to a manly woman crying over you in front of the hottest guy on the planet is a bit awkward. My best friend is the only sober one among us so she gets stuck with driving and then unloading the horses and the lesbian. She is not a happy camper at this point but the rest of us are too drunk to care.

We unload the magical ponies and the drunken bawling carriage driver and head back to my friend's house. We are lip locked again and the chamber is loaded. Our friends decide that we are way too drunk to drive which I agreed with, after the ten bottles of wine we consumed, so they put us on an air mattress on the floor in the living room. At this point you are probably thinking, what's so bad about this hookup it sounds pretty awesome except for the weird lesbian appearing out of nowhere with a team of white horses to drive you and your Prince Charming around. Well, just wait cause it is about to get messy.

Now it's around 4 a.m. we finally get our chance to be alone, although rumor has it things got pretty freaky in front of the friends I find out the next day. We get naked and I am pretty happy with the package when he starts making these really weird faces that just make me start laughing. He looks like he is blowing smoke rings, so I can't look at him.

The air mattress is like 50 percent blown up so we are sliding all over the thing and I am starting to get a little seasick. I try my best to ignore it and close my eyes and try and understand what he is saying to me in Spanish. It might have been move your elbow but it sounded really sexy.

I still felt the sick feeling in the pit of my stomach and it just was not going away and it didn't help he was tossing me around on that mattress like I was a blow up doll when out of nowhere I felt it rise all of his exquisite wine sprayed all over his luscious body along with a few curdles of goat cheese from earlier. I am mortified but he keeps going like this happens to him all the time or something maybe he was too drunk to notice but I tell him I have to stop and that I don't feel good.

I run into the bathroom and proceed to throw up again and again while swearing I will never drink wine again. I scramble to get my clothes and mumble something about having to go home and leave him wondering what the hell is wrong with American girls.

Size Matters

by Kimberly T. – Rosenberg, TX, age 25

My worst hookup was with this dude that my best friend and I had fought over in grade school. Well, we ended up working at the same restaurant in our late teens. We flirted all the time at work. So I asked him to a 4th of July party. I sucked him off and thought that would be the end of it.

Now, while I was down there, I was wasted as I usually was anytime a penis was involved. I didn't get a good look at the prize. A couple days later, though, he called me and wanted a booty call. I was bored, so I agreed to meet him at his place. I show up, oddly sober, and he leads me to this germ infested shitbox he called a room. Once there, he proceeds to rip my pants off, rip off his, and "bang" me like it was his job.

I put "bang" in quotes is because I couldn't feel a fucking thing. Apparently, he was done in 3 minutes and when he pulled out to cum, I was face-to-face with the most insignificant penis I have ever seen and

Chelsea Goldstein – www.chelseagoldstein.com

I am a fucking lesbian. We're talking, this thing was so small, I honestly remember thinking, "gee, that looks like my baby brother's thingy". No wonder I didn't gag while I was going down on him.

Jungle Juice

by Brooke J. – Raleigh, NC, age 25

When I was about 18, I was at this house party. I drank an obscene amount of Jungle Juice and somehow managed to convince an equally inebriated frat boy to accompany me home. I think we fucked at least I am pretty sure we did. The whole nights a bit hazy, but I was told the next morning by both my roommates that we were so loud they couldn't sleep. I assume that means we did it. I highly doubt we were discussing politics that intensely. The pièce de résistance, though, is that sometime during our raucous night, my lover and I use that term loosely as I can't remember his name, let alone his face decided he needed to answer the call of nature all over the floor of my roomies bathroom. Not a single iota of piss actually made it into the toilet. And, after the ridiculous quantity of alcohol he must've consumed, it wasn't so surprising that there was a lot of piss. We're talking, like, standing water amounts of pee.

Chelsea Goldstein – www.chelseagoldstein.com

Nothing like cleaning up some random piss after a night of what I can only assume was lousy sex and too much liquor. Needless to say, I don't drink Jungle Juice anymore.

Taste

by Haley B. – Chicago, IL, age 24

There was one night where I blew one guy and then two hours later, fucked another. But I feel the better story is that of my first experience with a girl. So I am gay, but hadn't ever been with a girl. We go to this little shithole of a gay bar.

In my nervousness, I felt it necessary to inhale, like, 5 shots of tequila. And, before you ask, my clothes did come off. She took me into an equally shitty bathroom and proceeded finger fuck the straight girl right out of me. The second time she took me to the bathroom 10 minutes later I learned that the bitch had a mouth like a fucking Hoover.

The slutty part comes in because a.) I only met her a week prior and b.) Her boyfriend who was with us told me later that he could taste me on her. Maybe that makes her a slut.

Cocaine

by Margaret B. – Nashville, TN, age 25

I haven't told anyone this story, but I just got back from Vegas and I figured you were the best person to confess to. While we were there my longtime friend Amanda and I were hanging out at the hotel bar watching Asian tourists singing karaoke. As funny as it was, we could only handle about 20 minutes of it and started talking to these English guys close to us.

Turns out that they were about 20 years older than us and I am 24, but they were adorable, had cute accents, and had cocaine. I had never tried it before, but I figured Vegas was the best time to try a little summer skiing.

The night was a blast, we went to a strip club, drank all night, and I really needed to get laid. Daniel was cute in 20 years older than me kind of way, so I decided to let him up to my room for a little you know what.

We had been doing coke all night, and had been drinking, and I was super excited to finally get laid after all that. He was going down on me, and then sort of stopped, and kept going. I can understand a little break, so I didn't really say anything. A few seconds later it he stopped again and I looked down and saw that his eyes were closed. That asshole actually fell asleep while eating my va-jay-jay. I'm not tooting my own horn, but I know damn well that I'm fun in bed. Particularly while being good head.

He later claimed to be a narcoleptic, but really, how often do you meet a drug toting, cradle robbing, narcoleptic British man in Vegas? Maybe I was boring, but I'm going to run with my dignity and believe he was a narcoleptic.

Mouth

by Brandi W. – Berkeley, CA, age 24

I was dating this guy a couple years ago and for New Years Eve he was spending the night at my house with my family. He forgot his pajamas so we went back to his house and his parents were going to a New Years party, leaving the house empty.

Figuring the dumbass locked the door after his parents left starting fooling around with him. I was giving him head when I hear his mom say, "what are you two doing?" Instead of playing it off cool, I look up, wipe my mouth, and stared. That was six years ago, and to this day I have not lived that moment down, but at least it has made a good story for us.

Piston

by Michelle T. – Clemson, SC, age 25

Let me preface the story by giving you some background on your new favorite best friend. I am 25, work in Corporate America, and my parents and those who do not know me best think I am a perfect angel. To those who know me best, I am a grade a girl next door slut who loves to booze. I am a good slut though the kind who people actually like and do not feel like they need to wear a full body condom when sitting next to.

My nickname is the PISTON. This started back when I was 18 years old by a group of guys who pretty much ran a train on me. Since then, I have embraced the name and it has become my drunk and slutty girl name. If the Piston is coming out, a good time is guaranteed to be had by all. Oh, and my best friend's "name" is the Demon. The piston and the demon sound like a good time.

After a good night of boozing and pistonish behavior, I can home drunk and alone. My ex boyfriend called we hook up occasionally and he is constantly in pursuit of my ass. It is not the best sex ever, but it works in a jam. Therefore, I decided to allow him to make the hour long drive to my house at 4:00 AM. He came, I rocked his world, and we went to sleep. At 8:30 AM, I was awoken by a call from another ex. I forgot that I had talked to him the night before and we made a date for him to come to my house in the morning for breakfast, some afternoon sex, and a game of dominos. At this point, I took a minute to think, "Do I want another round of mediocre sex with the man currently in my bed, or would I like to have round two with the ex on the phone?"

I choose option 2. At this point, Option 1 is still asleep in my bed and is hearing me place my breakfast order. I tell Option 2 I will see him in 30 minutes and hang up. Option 1 asks who is coming over for breakfast. I tell him my ex boyfriend is coming over and he needs to leave. I could tell that he was irritated that he drove an hour, fucked for two hours, slept for one, and had to leave my bed immediately without any AM sex. His response? He trics to have sex with me before he leaves.

At this point, I have about a 10 minute window before Option 2 arrives, and didn't want to cut it close. I told Option 2 that I couldn't be freshly sexed for the next guy and that he needed to leave. I quickly hopped in the shower, washed off the sex from the night before, straightened my bed, put on fresh lingerie, and was waiting half asleep in bed when option 2 came walking through the door with Starbucks in hand and ready to get down!

High Five

by Jenna W. – Tuscaloosa, AL, age 25

After a good night of boozing and slutty behavior, I can home drunk, but with a man this time. My roommate stayed at the bar and I sent her the old DND (Do Not Disturb) text. Since she LOVES to come and jump in my bed when she comes home hammered to try to engage in the most non-sexual lesbian behavior imaginable. Anyway, back to the story.

The dude and I start to get down and it was the most amazing sex I have had in two years. Huge penis, kind of rough, and he knew exactly what to do. I think that's what happens when two whores hook up. I didn't realize until now, but all the stories about how sex is so amazing when you are in love are complete Bullshit. I can't believe my mom told me such lies. The truth is that the more sex both parties have had with as many people as possible, the better.

I hear the cab pull up to drop my roommate and her drunken entourage off. I don't have a lock on my door it is an open door policy here, and I immediately knew that someone would walk thru my door to find me and the sex god in all of our naked glory. Plus, I had already cum, so I was ok with making him cease and desist for a moment. He was still on top of me with his penis halfway in and I pulled the sheet over us. No more than two seconds later, my door flies in and one of my good guy friends walks in demanding to be introduced because he could hear how much we were enjoying ourselves from the cab all of my windows were open. He walks over, shakes the sex god's hand and gives him a high five. He then begged to see my boobs, and after about two minutes, he turns and leaves. Sex god and I get back to business, and my drunken friend returns, but with another friend this time. I was close to cuming again, and decided that it wasn't worth stopping, so we continued with our business. The guys stood there for a minute, said what's up, jumped on my bed, and then ran out all while we continued with our business. The night continued with hours of amazing sex, followed by a few hours of sleep. I work up at about 8 and immediately decided that I was done with Sex god.

While I am a fan of sex, I am not a fan of cuddling, and definitely not a fan of hanging out for any longer than necessary to make the kill. Sex god was tired and in the mood to cuddle. I felt like I was suffocating. I was hot and tired, and didn't want to be touched unless it was by a penis in my puss. I woke him up, made up some BS story about how I had to be somewhere, gathered his things and showed him the door. The door shut, I locked it, and immediately got back in bed to dream about my next conquest.

Italian Fairy Tale

by Whitney C. – Lincoln, NE, age 27

I just got back from Italy. I won this trip and saw on the itinerary that we would have a driver. I thought, Please God, let this driver be hot! And so my friend and I finally get to Italy after being on a plane for 13 hours. Our plane was late so, of course, the driver wasn't there. I had to call the hotel and ask where our fucking driver was. And he finally came to pick us up. Can I say that this Italian god looked just like Daniel Craig from Casino Royale. Plus he was a really sharp dresser. He was wearing dress pants, a button up shirt with a fucking vest over it. Who does that in America?

The next day he took us to Chianti for wine tasting. We asked him to come drink with us and he said he was not allowed in his fine Italian accent. Drool. Apparently the Police are a little strict about alcohol in the system and driving. He asked if he could take me out to show some of the countryside. I agreed. I honestly wanted to go check out the Italian countryside in his Benz. I didn't know I should have shaved and put on matching underwear.

So he picks me up outside the view of the hotel so he can't get fired. And were off. He points out various Italian landmarks, the Palazzos, Duomos and Cathedrals. He bitches about the Italian President and we talk about American movies as well. He asks me if I want to see some olive trees. Hell yes, I do. So we drive up to this olive grove. It's fucking gorgeous! And he parks his Mercedes Benz between two olive trees and leans over and starts kissing me. He's all tongue. He grabs my hand and puts it on his crotch so I can start unbuttoning. And I oblige. He takes off my shirt and we know where this is going so he pulls me across, out of the driver door and we stumble to the back of the van. I get pushed on the seat. There is a door handle in my neck and the shoulder rest on my back. He hurriedly takes off his pants and his schlong is HUGE. As he looks at me and says, You like? I think this is going to hurt. After two hours of positions I've never done and car parts where they were never meant to be, we were done.

This short, Italian driver had way more spunk than I had originally thought. Most American guys can last about 30 minutes and they're done. Not this guy. I was the one thinking, is he done yet? I now think all Italian guys have huge schlongs too. They don't try to hide it in saggy American type jeans but wear tight threads to say, Hey you. Check this shit out. They also kiss hard. I made out with three Italian guys on the five day trip and all of them were balls to the wall tongue in your throat.

That night, I slept and did no sight seeing with my friend. I had bruises down my back from the van and was sore. He wore my ass out, correction: He did not wear my ass out, though he tried to a few times. Viva Italia!

My Bra

by Monica M. – Houston, TX, age 39

I was 17 young and horny. I was dating this sailor guy, who was stationed on their ship. It was cold out and we just wanted to cuddle. So I snuck him in my house and down the basement we went. I was still a virgin but I love to fool around.

At that age, sex was equal to dry humping and French fucks. Things got little hot and heavy after getting numb from dry humping we moved onto the French fuck position. I was wearing this one black bra that I loved. It had clasped in the front, but that day it kept coming undone so I pinned it.

As he was all into stroking his penis between my tits, and squeezing them together, out of nowhere, he starts squirming around, and screaming and yelping like a little girl. I am trying to get out from under him, and he keeps pushing me down and squeezing my tits even harder.

I had no clued what the hell he was trying to do, or what he wanted to do to me. I was so young and started to freak out thinking I'm going to get raped so I started punching him even harder and pushing myself out from under him. I was in such a panic, I wasn't really listening to him then I realized he's screaming about "something" and being "stuck in him".

I COMPLETELY Forgot about the Pin! It had come undone and was jammed right through his penis! Along with his junk being constricted between a set of tits and a bra. I hear my mother yelling down asking me if I am okay. I'm trying to desperately have him stop screaming so I can yell up to my mom that I was okay and had just stepped on a nail. And PREY that she doesn't come down.

Finally we got his cock released and had to wait over three long and uncomfortable hours for my mother to go to sleep so that I can sneak him up from the basement and out the door. That is one prick that seriously literally got pricked. Needless to say I never heard from him again.

My New Watch

by Chelsea S. – Brooklyn, NY, age 36

I had known this one guy for years, but were not daily friends. After bumping into each other at various lounges we finally hooked up. I was so crocked that night that I knew I was not looking all that pretty in the AM. So as soon as I woke up, I figured I'd get my shit and leave.

I then heard footsteps and started scrambling quietly for my clothes and jewelry in the dark. I couldn't find a damn thing and didn't want to wake up the guy or be heard. I would have been mortified being caught by his roommate, so I grabbed any shirt on the floor and all jewelry on the end table and skipped out the back door.

I did the walk of shame for 5 blocks looking disheveled in a t-shirt that read "Born to Rock" but surprisingly sporting a watch that not only wasn't my famous $50 rip-off Gucci bracelet watch, but a really nice buckle watch that fit me perfectly.

A few weeks later, I went out in my new found

watch, and bumped into the guy. Of course, as with all initial post encounters, I didn't know what to say and belted out, "Thanks for my new watch!' Not realizing that he wasn't alone or that he was even attached. I hear his "girlfriend" come out from nowhere shouting, "What's this bitch doing with my watch?!"

That was my queue for me, my cocktail, and my new watch to jet out of there. For weeks and weeks after that, I was tortured by him on getting this watch back. He called his girlfriend called and txt her friend's called and txt. I blocked all their numbers but their desperation piqued my interest in finding out about this watch. Months went by, and had bumped into him again, girlfriend-less and watch-less.

Three Little Pigs

by Angela A. – Philadelphia, PA, age 38

Tom, Joe and Ace, three fraternity boys that went to college with me, moved off campus during our senior year. Always an issue, nobody wanted to purchase more paper products other words more toilet paper when they run out in college. These boys were no different. Once they ran out of toilet paper, they used paper towels, napkins, until these were gone too. Once the paper products were exhausted, they take a shower. Basically these guys decided the only time to take a poop was pre-shower.

One night, a wasted Ace came home and found himself taking a king sized dump and was too drunk, tired and lazy to shower himself. He decided the best way to handle this was to remove the t-shirt he was wearing and have at it. He proceeded to soil his clothing, crumpled it in a ball and staggered to bed, tossing the shirt in a darkened corner of his messy room.

How could this be a hook-up story, you ask? Enter my friend Angela. A while after Aces t-shirt incident and let's hope, a much-needed trip to K-Mart for paper products, Angela was at a party beer goggling and had her eye on Ace. Angela and Ace spent much of the evening flirting over a mean game of quarters, followed by Asshole, and then Ace walked her home to his apartment for a magical, drunken hookup. This probably consisted of a limp dick too much booze, or maybe a really long, never-ending sex session ending in whiskey dick also too much booze for Ace and some chafing for Angela. So, once they were all partied out and sexed out, they had a quick cuddle around 4 a.m. Angela said to Ace, I need some pajamas. It is so cold. So Ace fumbled around the bed mattress, no box spring, in the middle of his bedroom floor, of course and found something for her to sleep in. They passed out, drooled off to sleep, and slept the night to early morning until 10. All the while, Ace dreaming he was a pig, in a sty, that reeked of shit.

When Ace awakened next to Angela, he was stricken by a pungent aroma. How does this cute girl smell so disgusting, he asked himself? He opened his eyes and saw Angela sleeping beside him in a rumpled t-shirt covered in his skid marks.

He then flashed back to several weeks earlier remembered a foggy explosion on the toilet, inappropriate wiping, oh shit. This girl is going to fucking kill me, he thought. A few seconds later, Angela woke up, snuggled up and one thing led to another. Ace that sneaky little devil managed to get her out of her shirt and had sex with her again let's hope it was proper this time. By some miracle, Angela never knew she spent the night sleeping in Aces shit stains.

Eventually the story came out because all the guys knew about it and it did finally get back to Angela. Five years after we graduated, on their wedding night, we decorated their car with shaving cream, condoms, the usual, and a t-shirt painted with brown marks to resemble there poop stains.

Sailor

by Cynthia P. – Phoenix, AZ, age 27

So my friends and I started an organization at my school. Basically we take a trip once a semester to somewhere cool. Our very first trip was Chicago. I had never been there before and I was super excited. The waivers that were signed for school only had two conditions: no cohabitation and no drinking. I am known for following the rules. Of course I end up breaking both.

It was Saturday night, and before heading off to Navy Pier for the night my friends and I decided to kick off the evening with some very classy bagged wine. After knocking back a few we headed off to navy pier and headed to the Pier. We decided to go to the haunted house. While a bunch of floozies dressed in "scary" costumes tried to intimidate us before entering we just laughed. Behind us a bunch of young guys in uniform inched their way up to our group. They introduced themselves as navy seals, and offered their services to help us through the maze. Afterward we decided to go on the famous ferris wheel. Luckily for us the seals decided to inform us that we were not allowed to go on the ride unless we had a navy seal with us. So the tall blonde, with blue eyes and a southern accent offered my friends their pick. Afterwards I was left with the shockingly good looking red neck.

During the wait for the ferris wheel I listened to him go on and on about being from Louisiana. Before I knew my friend started speaking in a southern accent as well. It has become clear that she had the same talent as Madonna speaking in many accents.

The time came and each of us went off into a cart with our respective sailors and my friends enjoyed each others company. I spent the ride being terrified by heights and cuddled to death by "My Favorite Sailor". Afterward the sexy version of "larry the cable guy", his friends, and myself along with my friends payed a Hugh Hefner look a like to drive us back to the hotel room. Eventually his friends left.

My friend decided to sleep on the floor out of fear of what Coyboy and I would be doing. My other friends fell asleep. I went to bed fully aware of the fact that this guy was looking for something. Every two hours I would be woken by "Big N Rich" because he would not stop fondling me. I would fool around and then try to go back to sleep. I did not care about his six pack abs and his stories of hanging out with Britney Spears, at the time Britney was in turmoil and it was not someone to brag about okay?! I wanted him gone. Especially when his "one eyed snake" was a little too close to my back door.

By the time the morning came I woke up happy as could be because I would get this douche out of my hotel room. I even resorted to singing "In The Navy" by the village people to hurry him along since he had previously mentioned he hated that song. I wanted to go back home where the guys knew where the "hot pocket" was and how to leave me the hell alone.

Made in the USA
Lexington, KY
28 December 2009